Towards Reconciliation

Informal in tone and remarkably accessible, this book makes a compelling case that the reconciliatory potential of Christian faith can't be realized until and unless we have a theory of scapegoating. Masterfully presenting René Girard's fundamental anthropology as the definitive resource for this effort, Gifford weaves references to film and literature as well as to biblical passages into a narrative that traces a sure path from toxic to reconciling relationships. The definitive guide to Girard for 21st century readers.

Martha J. Reineke, PhD
Professor of Religion, University of Northern Iowa
President, Colloquium on Violence and Religion

This book addresses the apocalyptic panic of our time, manifest particularly in religion-inspired terrorism. Amid the blame-shifting responses, the lure of identity politics and the failure of secularised societies to understand either the danger or the redemptive force of religion, Paul Gifford's book offers clarity and hope, introducing René Girard's revolutionary understanding of the connection between violence and sacred and how this is progressively undermined and finally overthrown in the texts of Western Christianity.

Angela Tilby
Canon Emeritus, Christ Church, Oxford

I'm so glad that a wider readership can now join those listeners in Coventry who were lucky enough to hear the original lectures. This book offers a stunningly complete overview of René Girard's thought and shows how to begin applying his insights – so much wisdom and finesse in these interpretations. And the range of examples offered is just wonderful! I'd never heard of Croghan man, but what a perfect find.

James Alison
Catholic Priest and Theologian

Towards Reconciliation
Understanding Violence and the Sacred after René Girard

Paul Gifford

James Clarke & Co

James Clarke & Co
P.O. Box 60
Cambridge
CB1 2NT
United Kingdom

www.jamesclarke.co
publishing@jamesclarke.co

Hardback ISBN: 978 0 227 17708 2
Paperback ISBN: 978 0 227 17707 5
PDF ISBN: 978 0 227 90709 2
ePub ISBN: 978 0 227 90710 8
Kindle ISBN: 978 0 227 90711 5

British Library Cataloguing in Publication Data
A record is available from the British Library

First published by James Clarke & Co, 2020

Copyright © Paul Gifford, 2020

All rights reserved. No part of this edition may be reproduced, stored electronically or in any retrieval system, or transmitted in any form or by any means, electronic, mechanical, photocopying, recording, or otherwise, without prior written permission from the Publisher (permissions@jamesclarke.co).

For René Girard
(1923-2015)

in affectionate memory

Contents

Introduction ... ix

1. What Is 'Sacred Violence'? ... 1
2. Violent Origins, Origins of Violence ... 21
3. Girardian 'Founding Murder' ... 35
4. Violence, the Archaic Sacred and Judaeo-Christian Revelation ... 58
5. Passion, Resurrection – and How We Come by Reconciliation ... 81
6. Taking Thought for Reconciliation ... 105

Appendix: 'From Animal to Human', 'On Religion' – Conversations with René Girard ... 123
Cited Texts and Further Reading ... 139
Index ... 143

Illustration

Artist's reconstruction of the world's oldest known temple, Göbekli Tepe (c. 9,600 BCE). ... 53
Courtesy of National Geographic

Introduction

The origins and background of this slim volume call for a few words of explanation. My title will surprise or puzzle a number of readers, not least in the reference made to a French-American thinker, influential in Europe and across the Atlantic, who died quite recently without, as yet, having become well-read, well-understood or well-accepted in this country. Among these necessary preliminaries, I would wish to accommodate some important thanks and acknowledgements.

This book began life as a series of four Lenten lectures given at Coventry Cathedral (St Michael's House) in 2016. The invitation came from Coventry's (then) Canon for Reconciliation, Rev Dr Sarah Hills, who knew something of the – otherwise little known – part played by Girard's thinking in the Northern Ireland peace process.

I am grateful for her prompt understanding that the cause of Reconciliation needed all the help it could get; and for her discernment in suspecting that, in Girard, it just might come to discover a framing theory capable of bringing new light, momentum and direction to Coventry's long-standing and established Ministry of Reconciliation.

'Theory' of any kind, tends, at first sight, to appear discouraging or dislikeable to British instincts of empirical sense-making and pragmatic muddling through; and, certainly, the precedents of 'French Theory' or 'Critical Theory' illustrated in the latter third of the twentieth century are – as Girard himself vigorously argued – not always inviting or impressive. However, the point about a 'theory' is that, well done, it can simplify and unify cogently complex aspects of reality. It brings difficult and obscure phenomena into manageable focus so that they become amenable to human thought and action. That is a highly desirable asset in the field of reconciliation.

Sarah Hills could not, at that time of her invitation, have known that the death of René Girard (intervening as we spoke in November 2015) would trigger, in Europe and the United States of America, a series of 'after René Girard' books, together with a rediscovery of this thinker's often neglected writings on religion. My thanks to Sarah are all the warmer for her unknowing. Without her generous and far-seeing invitation to a retired professor of French, recently dropped into Coventry Diocese from St Andrews in Scotland, this book would have found no occasion to exist; it might not have come to be.

In one sense, however, the book of the lectures is indeed a function of what was *not* then known. It echoes, at a more modest level, such works of recapitulation, review and re-evaluation as Grant Kaplan's indispensable *René Girard, Unlikely Apologist: Mimetic Theory and Fundamental Theology* (2016) and Bernard Perret's admirable *Penser la foi chrétienne après René Girard* (2018).[1] It offers, in other words, to mediate for British readers, at a more introductory level, the job done by these works in, respectively, the United States and France.

It is not always the case, of course, that public lectures can (or should) survive their oral presentation. In this case, they did and have; with a quarter (or so) of new material added, while still conserving something – I hope – of the immediacy and freshness of the original face-to-face occasion.

The reason for their surviving is not far to seek. The intellectual electricity generated transcended that original context and continues to do so. How can one begin to address, let alone resolve, problems that have not been adequately explored and understood? And who, then, will decipher for us the seemingly bottomless enigma of 'violence and the sacred'? That question had particular resonance in 2016, in the context created by the alarming brutalities of so-called Islamic State (IS) in Syria and elsewhere; but it was – and it remains – a question pertinent to the modern world as a whole; it was and remains everybody's problem.

I had by the time of that invitation become convinced that René Girard, the Stanford-based, French-American, fundamental anthropologist and culture theorist, had the lion's share of the available research-based insight and the best overview (or 'theory') – the theory best capable of accommodating and interacting with other 'best insights' of all sorts and from many quarters.

---

1. Details of this and other such works are given in Cited Texts and Further Reading at the end of this volume.

It had not always been so. When I read, in French, his first groundbreaking essay in cultural anthropology of 1972, *Violence and the Sacred*, I found it too novel, too disconcerting, and insufficiently 'resolved' in its strangeness. I was deeply suspicious, also – along with most other British readers at the time – of the foundational idea that human culture, including religion, had developed out of, and as a protection against, human violence.

Fifteen years later, I returned to Girard, feverishly turning the pages of his Socratic dialogue and intellectual thriller, *Things Hidden from the Foundation of the World*. Only then did 'the penny drop'. This moment of illumination happened, as I recall, under canvas, as the skies above our family tent opened and my children, cooped up within that fragile refuge on the Languedoc coast, ran amok, all unheeded, around me . . . and my wife despaired of masculine-kind!

I went on to do what precious few of Girard's English critics have since done: namely, read all his other writings and understand his way of thinking. I discovered a rich and unknown country of the mind. Here was the 'one that got away', certainly, from the enclosure of minds within the Mind and from endless self-referentiality;[2] but here, too, was the French theorist who was no longer just French; who wrote and thought against the grain of all other 'French theory' (which is far better known in this country); and yet, this alternative theorist had actually enabled all their reputations to develop. It was Girard who, in 1966, co-hosted an international conference on 'The Languages of Criticism and the Sciences of Man', attended by all the stars of post-structuralism and of deconstruction: Barthes, Lacan, Foucault, Goldmann, Paul de Man and Derrida (invited when Lévi-Strauss declined) et al. This much-remarked conference at the Johns Hopkins University in Baltimore, introduced 'French Theory' to a transatlantic English-speaking public – thereby provoking turbulent and heated debate and a spectacular turmoil over teaching programmes within many American universities. In later life, Girard was known to 'confess' – with a mischievous twinkle – to having 'brought the plague from Europe to America'.[3]

As far as our own English-speaking country is concerned, Girard's reputation never really surmounted the influential accident which

---

2. 'Mimetic desire is a realist theory which shows why human beings are incapable of realism' (Girard, VR [*La voix méconnue du réel*] 2001:207).
3. For the avoidance of doubt, 'plague', like 'flood', is, in Girard's thought, a significant metaphor for the contagion of violent strife, which is the direct referent of this remark.

meant that, commuting between his native France and his adoptive professional home of America, he regularly bypassed London, flying over or travelling around it.

Along with leading French philosopher Paul Ricœur, and other luminaries in many humanities disciplines, René Girard was, however, invited to the University of St Andrews as part of a public lecture and seminar series marking the bi-millennium (since published by Routledge under the title *2000 Years and Beyond* [Gifford et al. 2003]). It was one of only two or three such invitations he ever received to visit the UK. Eminent figures such as Paul Ricœur and Jürgen Moltmann, predictably drew to that particular event, from all over Scotland, huge audiences, whom they by no means disappointed; but it was a brilliant Girard, then at the height of his powers, who truly dazzled and fascinated his somewhat smaller ones. 'The best performance I have heard in over 30 years at St Andrews', said the then Berry Professor of English of the two-hour seminar, which followed on, a day later, from Girard's public lecture, and which I had the privilege of chairing.

Our acquaintance developed; and in 2007 I was invited to work with Girard, then emeritus Professor at Stanford, as Invited Scholar in his own Department of French and Italian. Having myself retired in the interval, and presented Girard for an honorary degree at St Andrews (with support from the Schools of Divinity, of Philosophy and Social Anthropology, as well as of Modern Languages), I returned to California, as elected Visiting Research Fellow of the Girardian foundation 'Imitatio', based at Stanford University.

Despite being, in Girardian terms, something of a 'labourer of the eleventh hour', I became then one of a tiny handful of British scholars fortunate enough, in workshops and conferences over a considerable period, to have interacted closely with the alternative theorist.

Here, I would wish to register a deep debt of gratitude also to the insight and scholarship of many longer-established Girardian colleagues, encountered in that place and time, who have likewise advanced my understanding of the depth, range and prodigious potential of mimetic theory. Chief among these are Paul Dumouchel, James Alison, Benoît Chantre, Jean-Pierre Dupuy, Andrew McKenna, Wolfgang Palaver, Michael Kirwan, Jean-Michel Oughourlian, Martha Reineke, Sandor Goodhart and Pierpaolo Antonello;[4] the last-named

---

4. Pierpaolo Antonello is Reader in modern Italian literature and culture at the University of Cambridge and Fellow of St John's College. With René Girard and João Cezar de Castro Rocha he co-authored *Evolution and Conversion: Dialogues*

being the Cambridge-based co-editor, with me, of the two books (2015a and 2015b) that emerged in those years from the three conferences, organised between 2009 and 2013 at Cambridge and Stanford, around the theme of 'Darwin and Girard'.

It is a considerable fact about studies in Girardian mimetic theory that they represent an ongoing collective enterprise, engaging many disciplines, and addressing many topics pursued by researchers of diverse sensibilities and mindsets all over the world. This fraternal diaspora is very loosely organised in a – sometimes dynamic and sometimes unstable – ellipse. It turns around the twin focal points represented by the 'Imitatio' foundation, on the one hand, and, on the other, by the standing Colloquium on Violence and Religion (COV&R).[5] The rewarding aspect of this unusual constellation of researchers and seekers is, as one might imagine, its implied catholicity of mind, its rich human diversity and unfailing intellectual stimulus. The penalty is that not all Girardians think with the concise and modest brilliance of their original inspirer. Girard is often then misjudged by the dispersed order – and even by the lesser merit – of the ever-growing host of Girardians.

'It remains true that the reception – not infrequently, the non-reception – of Girard in the UK presents a special and interesting case of academic *mésestime*.[6] True: Girard's reputation was never easily or comfortably established anywhere: the interdisciplinary nature of his thought disconcerts many; so does its relentless focus and consistency – and its breadth of purview. His thrust is counter-cultural; and there must be discomfort where so many corporations and establishments are challenged, so many minds asked to turn around. The prophet always divides opinion and scandalises. Whatever seems powerfully prophetic to some will inevitably appear suspiciously marginal and irritatingly maverick to others. And yet the prophet opens ears and eyes to what is closest to us and to the things we most need to discover.

---

    on the Origins of Culture, and he is a member of the Research and Publications committees of 'Imitatio'.

5. As its website explains, this review has been devoted (since 1990) to 'Exploring, Critiquing and Developing Girard's Mimetic Theory', https://violenceandreligion.com. The Imitatio website (www.imitatio.org) has many brief videoclips in which Girard expounds key points of his theory.

6. One sign that the ice age may be yielding was the foundation of a new series devoted to Girard at the Bloomsbury Press under the title 'Violence and the Sacred'. The first volume, edited by Scott Cowdell, Chris Fleming and Joel Hodge was *Girard's Mimetic Theory Across the Disciplines* (2012).

It is in this larger context that I would wish to express my very warmest thanks to Dr Rowan Williams, currently Master of Madgalene College, Cambridge. He is well-placed to know why such *mésestime* occurs – also, and perhaps especially, in academe. He has used his considerable position and public influence generously, in giving play to promising theories, and their bearers; especially where they both attract stone-throwers and, as in this particular case, also make intelligible the phenomenon of stone-throwing (known, in the more violent forms it assumes in certain social and religious practices, as 'lapidation').

His support has been invaluable in introducing Girard to established opinion-formers in this country: by attending, while still at Lambeth, the first Darwin-Girard conference in Cambridge; and, subsequently, by prefacing the two Darwin-Girard books which appeared under the titles *Can We Survive Our Origins?* and *How We Became Human*. He also chaired *con brio* the book launch of the two Darwin-Girard titles at the Cambridge Festival of Ideas in October 2015.

More than that: the simple encouragement he has given has been sustaining. It derives from an idea I have come to share with him and which underlies the present book. Rowan Williams was among the very first to understand that a cogent theory of emissary victimisation (or 'scapegoating') is required in our twenty-first-century culture, if the Passion of Christ is to remain, in this time of interfaith and of no faith, universally accessible, and its true resonance and import discerned.

A serious piece of fundamental anthropology, in other words, is required to unlock the transformative and reconciliatory potential of the Christian faith itself. If the present book can contribute in any measure to meeting that strategic requirement of our times, it will have achieved its goal; its travelling will have been light, and its labour joyful.

My lively thanks go, finally, to two colleagues: Professor Ann Loades, CBE, who gave me good, crisp and stimulating theological advice; and Professor Brian Stimpson whose reactions helped define my sense of what, where and how much to explain.

The old adage is still true: for whatever defects remain, the responsibility is entirely mine.

1
What Is 'Sacred Violence'?

My general proposal in this short book is that we will come to be better reconcilers if we can manage to gain a sharper and more joined-up understanding of how human violence is linked to the sacred.

If I had advanced this proposal before the attack in 2001 on the twin towers in New York (the event known as 9/11), my guess is that it would have risked appearing eccentric. Few people, really, thought there *was* any link worth mentioning between human violence and the sacred ('whatever that might be').

It is certainly true that this latter word has virtually dropped out of academic anthropology in our own time, having been one of the keywords of that discipline in its glory days, during the first half of the twentieth century. Books on terrorism do still sometimes invoke the sacred, but without being very sure of how or when it should be used. Michael Burleigh, an eminent academic historian, used it his three-part history of politics and religion: *Sacred Causes* (2005 and 2007) and *Earthly Powers* (2006). However, when he came, in 2008, to write *Blood and Rage: A Cultural History of Terrorism*, the word sacred was dropped. Too difficult to manage, perhaps? Or perhaps that cause was not sacred to us – that is, to the 'us' likely to purchase the book; and who, among that public, was likely to know, reliably, what the sacred is, anyway? Yet, would there be any rage, or any blood, if it were not for the sacred cause which terrorists pursue; and the sacred intensity with which they pursue it?

Take the title of another book in this field, John Esposito's *Unholy War: Terror in the Name of Islam* (2002). Now that's a really excellent book, retracing, exactly and coolly, the rise in modern times, of a politically radicalised fundamentalism within Islam. Esposito rightly wants us to distinguish what's holy and what's unholy, first, to rebuke the claims of Islamist fundamentalists to be fighting what Muslims have very frequently called 'Holy War' (that expression is, of course, very much part of the history of Christendom also). Second, Esposito seeks to refute one of the first Western interviews in 1997 with Al Qaeda leader bin Laden broadcast on CNN News by that organisation's Security Analyst Peter Bergen (1997) and subsequently reproduced in the latter's book *Holy War, Inc.* (2001) (i.e. 'Incorporated') – Bergen's critical 'take' here being: this is basically a modern, secular, Western-inspired movement with a few Islamic religious trappings. Esposito objects squarely and properly to both these suggestions; but even he, I think, misses the deepest level of explanation by failing to see any daylight, any illuminating contrast, between the sacred and the holy.

In all this, the sacred looks a bit like what physicists refer to as dark matter. Plenty of it about, but our instruments can't quite get hold of it. No more in the cultural universe of mind-made – that is, human – things, than in nature's physical cosmos. We are only now beginning, perhaps, to wake up to the sacred, and to shed our reticence in facing up to all its implications. If, having been jerked awake by Islamist *jihad*, with its blood, its rage and its sacred cause, we now fail to 'make the hard yards' towards understanding this neglected category of things human, and fail to discern its deep-laid connection to human violence, then our reconciliation talk is likely to be unfocussed. It risks being a patchy empirical practice at best, deprived of the strong direction, discernment, consistency and effective focus that an appropriate theoretical understanding can bring. At worst, it risks becoming a blundering and talkative irrelevance. Reconciliation? Yes, of course: we all just love it. But, alas, sometimes in the mode of 'motherhood and apple pie'. Whereas, as Bonhoeffer pointed out, and as Coventry Cathedral, standing side by side with its own blitzed and blackened ruin, has paid dearly enough to remember well, there isn't any cheap grace.

So, here's the plan. I suggest we start work at once on that third term of my general title 'Towards Reconciliation: Understanding Violence and the Sacred'. Having got a handle on what we least understand and most leave out of account – namely, the sacred – we can then work our way, stage by stage, towards understanding sacred or sacral violence. That's what will help us know when, how, and even if, we can move forward in the underlying enterprise and mission of reconciliation.

There will be some merit, too, in discovering, as a function of the challenge it assumes, what reconciliation itself is and does, and why we need it.

* * *

'I'm often asked what I think of "the sacred". I usually answer: I don't know what it is!' I'm quoting Rowan Williams (no less), speaking socratically, tongue-in-cheek, at an event during the Cambridge University 'Festival of Ideas' of October 2015, where this notion came up. Those are wise words. The sacred is protean, like electricity: it takes multiple forms; it produces the most diverse and bewilderingly contradictory discourses of explanation; and, to boot, it generates in our modern secular culture, a 'don't go there' reaction of suspicion, irritated incomprehension and antipathy.

Given that elusive character, my best tactic will be to offer a series of glimpses of the sacred in action. My former colleagues in academe, those of them who are philosophers, at least, would no doubt have urged me to call this exercise 'a phenomenology of the sacred'. What I will say is that it's a DIY version of that very fine thing – which is as much as I can manage – and it is offered here because it will speak more immediately to an English-speaking audience than the more characteristically French approach and mindset, prepared by Descartes and the Structuralists of the 1960s, which we shall hear about in our next chapter from René Girard. (In Girard, that inheritance is handled with the intuitional flair and sensitivity of the great novelist Proust, with whom Girard also has affinities.) I hope this move will not give rise to confusion: Girard is the one with the real insight, as will quickly become clear; but there is an introductory job of cultural translation and empirical recognition to be achieved first, before we can benefit from his insights.

With this brief prologue, let me simply jump in at the deep end. We recall the episode, in the Old Testament, of the *Akedah*, that is, the 'binding' of Isaac (Genesis 22:9). A call or duty in the order of things sacred, is, seemingly, laid upon the patriarch Abraham: he's called to sacrifice his son.

Now, if we are at all anthropologically minded, we prick up our ears at this: because that sacred duty allows us to identify the implicit context in time and space: it sends us back to the era of human blood sacrifice, specifically, of bloody child sacrifice, a practice which Israel indeed encountered in the land of Canaan, and in counter-distinction to which, the religion of Israel is itself emerging and evolving. (Look, for example, at Leviticus 18:21 and Deuteronomy 18:9-14 – the Revised Standard Version of the Bible has a section headed 'Child Sacrifice, Divination and Magic Prohibited'.)

A call that is sacred binds both the victim and the human subject who is charged to do God's received or supposed will. In this case – here is the emerging Hebraic novelty – Abraham is the agent of the divine purpose, through whom passes God's promise of blessing for all of humankind. In order to transmit that blessing he must have a descendency; he must have that long-delayed and much expected son, the very one who – this is the knot of the story – is apparently demanded as sacrificial victim.

Hence an exquisite ambiguity, a baffling problem. On the one hand, the sacred call is the imperative and all-overriding voice of God (the sacred always implies 'absolute, non-negotiable'). On the other, it signifies the appalling horror of the knife that kills. To decide, as Abraham does, to sacrifice his son, is both a horrifically costly offering of faith-obedience and, in good etymology, a cutting-away of Israel's covenant promise itself. More than mere 'survival', it is Israel's hope of salvation, and ours, that is at stake. This act is, or it would have been, if it had come to pass, sacred violence; but here, in this haunting story, sacred violence is being presented in its very sharpest and most problematic profile.

How can God really desire or countenance the sacrificial killing of the bearer of the divine promise? That's the central paradox. It is resolved, albeit incompletely, in the story. God, it turns out, provides the 'proper' scapegoat victim for sacrifice: the ram caught by its horns in the thicket. He had, so the text leads us to suppose, intended this outcome from the beginning: Abraham's faith was being tried. However, we glimpse here obliquely a remembrance of something else as well: namely, the modulation of the institution itself of sacrifice – the passage from human sacrifice to animal sacrifice within the religion of Israel. We see also how that modulation allows the writers of this story to escape from the worst 'cutting edge', so to speak, of sacred violence (it is not always known that the English word 'scapegoat' connotes, etymologically, an *escape* goat). Meanwhile, the more subtle notion that Abraham is being tested in his faith commitment, eases the advent of a revisionist theology; everyone's sacred is not necessarily, it seems, the accurate or adequate expression of Israel's high and holy God.

Abraham is unbound, let off the hook, so to speak, along with Isaac; and so is Israel; and all three become better bonded to God, as he is truly. (That's how the story turns out in the telling, i.e. in retrospective interpretation.) Not only so; but, as Austrian Catholic theologian Wolfgang Palaver points out, this story of the 'transcended human sacrifice' marks, along with the historical rejection of that particular institution, the acceptance of the 'divine' value of human being as such (Palaver 2009: 29-65).

What is residually problematic, of course, is the changing representation and image of God. What certainly remains unresolved is the gap between how we feel and perceive divine transcendence and, on the other hand, how God really is, ultimately, in Himself. That indeterminate and potentially vast gap, is here bridged by one little step of understanding, a tiny step taken empirically, by trial and error, in human time. This world, it seems, is the place where the will of God is not known with certainty, not infallibly done; where it can be and often will be, monstrously misconstrued and misrepresented, caricatured and violently flouted. Where the imperative of survival may be at odds with the necessities of salvation. The same world, in fact, as is recognised in the Gospel: 'Thy Kingdom come . . . on earth, as it is in Heaven'.

However, have we not thereby recognised also the gap of cognitive understanding, of spiritual ambiguity and human uncertainty, within which the sacred operates and within which any number of human and cultural factors, themselves changing in space and in time, have play and hold sway? We begin to see why the human sense of the sacred can and does change, and change with protean variety, in time and space; how it can even change valency – here, from something morally positive, i.e. blood sacrifice, in its primitive acceptance, is God-given, good and due, to something morally negative ('No, God does not desire sacrifice, not if by sacrifice is understood the bloody immolation of a child scapegoat victim').

Then, however, if that is true, can we not just as well envisage the case in which this shift of moral valency and perspective does not happen; or, if it does, is obscured by a subsequent regression to a more primitive understanding? Witness Islamist fundamentalism; witness Islamic State. Muslims can, of course, reject IS and most do; but it is a mistake to pretend that IS isn't a religiously inspired, millenarian group, with a recognisably Islamic imprint. Anjem Choudary, London's most notorious, and currently imprisoned, defender of IS, has said quite openly that crucifixions and beheadings are 'sacred requirements'. Princeton-based academic specialist of mediaeval Islam, Bernard Haykel agrees: 'Slavery, crucifixions and beheadings are not something that freakish jihadists are cherry-picking from mediaeval Islamic tradition.' IS fighters are 'smack in the middle of the mediaeval tradition and are bringing it wholesale into the present day'; 'They are authentic throwbacks to early Islam and are faithfully reproducing its norms of war.'[1]

Of course, the way we assess this continuity is still subject to the distinction we have just established in relation to Judaeo-Christian tradition: the distinction between a religious dimension and a socio-cultural order. The origin of this distinction lies so deep and is so aboriginal that lines of distinction are all but impossible to draw with any authority. Until, that is, and unless, we have an account of the genesis of religion and of the relation of religion to revelation. It is in this zone of deepest unsightedness and obscurity that Girard will be seen to bring invaluable light.

We can see, at least that the *Akedah* is important to us all because it points to a parting of the ways in the religious development of humankind as such. One way leads to a critical, contextualised and emergentist view of the religious source tradition; the other to an unmoving, unbending adherence to an absolutist sacrality. From that point on, most of us will wish to distinguish between the (human) sacred and the (truly, intrinsically) holy. That is a distinction of extreme significance; and it becomes entirely crucial, I suggest, when we are proposing to speak carefully, rather than quickly and ill-advisedly, about the involvement in human violence of religion.

We can indeed perhaps sum up the argument thus far by saying: there are two doors marked 'Swift Exit from this Topic'. I hope we shall avoid taking either of them. One, if we are Muslims, will have written on it: 'IS is totally un-Islamic; it has nothing whatever to do with Islam'. The other, if we are Jewish or Christian, is like unto it: 'Sacred violence is quite foreign to our religion; it has no part in our faith-tradition or our history'.

* * *

'An organised public cult in the order of the sacred' – I think that's probably what most anthropologists these days would agree to mean by the word religion. Organised means that some specific content, some

---

1. 'What is the Islamic State?', WebPost of investigative journalist Jaclyn Skurie, 17 November 2015.

form of ritual procedure and some significant mind-shape has been imposed on something more spontaneous or immediate than went before, and out of which the organised cult has developed. It is likely that the sacred will, when the sciences of anthropology, ethnology and comparative religion have caught up with it adequately, prove to have been – and, obscurely, to be still – the matrix from which originally emerged all of the unnumbered and multifarious varieties of the human phenomenon we are content, usually unthinkingly, to call religion. At which point, we might come to recognise, without the reflex of incredulity this possibility often evokes in our contemporaries, why that category of things human is very much with us still.

It is sufficiently clear, at all events, that the sacred is a proto-form of human spirituality, anticipating for long eons the organised cults we call religion. Its earliest expressions may have been very basic indeed; so basic that it may have been no more than the most intuitional group understanding that flickers invisibly between us, making us of one mind – binding us together, even as it binds us to and bonds us with an immediately felt mystery going beyond ourselves, registering indistinctly some transcendence. We think here, for instance, of the archaic-sacral veneration for blood, for fire.

What binds and bonds us still today are the 'sacralities' we share. If we doubt that, or fail to see what it means, we might try observing the playing of national anthems at rugby world cup finals, or at similarly big occasions and solemn gatherings. Look at those virile heroes of the fifteen-a-side oval-shaped ball, lined up before the match, personally delegated to carry the torch for their nation, bearing witness, before a massed audience of sports lovers in the stadium and worldwide, to the deeper and older thing that lifts them towards supreme effort and glory. Watch the closed hand held over the heart; see how the faces struggle to retain composure – deeply breathing, facial muscles frozen, eyes closed, lip quivering. Our heroes are close to tears, mouthing the words that many are unable to sing, invaded and taken over as they are by the 'god' of sacred emotion.

Or think of the dark charisma, fiercer and more brutal in feeling, of Hitler's Nuremberg rallies (recorded for posterity in newsreels and in Leni Riefenstahl's film *The Triumph of the Will*). That darker sacrality is distilled out of the torchlit procession, the chants, the slogans, the hypnotic cadences of urgent and rasping speech, organising the darkness, imprinting the ardent passivity of the listeners. This is an elaborately staged, ideologically orchestrated, pagan liturgy. Yes, the sacred varies in content and ethos – here, it communes in the Will to Power incarnate in the *Führer* and magnified, in a feedback loop, by his entranced and yielding audience. However, it is, in all of us, the psychic or spiritual tissue of group understanding, complicity, intimacy; it is the most immediate experience of community, of communion – hence, also, of collective identity as such; in short, the immediate and innermost electricity of us-ness, exalted by a sense of transcendence, i.e. of extra- or super-us-ness.

In content and tenor, the sacred always was, and still is, ambiguous: now a sort of benign white magic, and now positively demonic. It's decidedly black in the work of one modern atheistic thinker, close to the Surrealist movement. Writing in the 1920s and 1930s, Georges Bataille accuses Christianity of catastrophically domesticating the sacred; it has drowned our sense of common spiritual tissue and, particularly, it has extinguished that primordial contact with life, he says, by dousing it in a bland and benign therapy of white magic, thus opening a door to secularisation. Under this name, he describes a process of desacralisation evacuating that fearsome thrill of existing in a dangerous cosmos, insulating us from that primitive electric charge of the erotic life-current pulsing in everything, and thus opening the door to utilitarian values and to the pragmatic, down-to-earth prosaic realisms of the century (remember, the word secular, is related to fr. *siècle* < lat. *saeculum*). His idea is that our Western culture has thrown out the baby (the sacred) with the bathwater (he means organised, public religion – in practice, for Bataille and most Frenchmen, the Catholic Church).

Bataille then explores the erotic thrill to be rediscovered in the transgression of religious commandments and civilised proprieties. His theme is sacred or sacral violence, which is always a violation of individual bodies and of moral norms. It involves a tearing apart of our being, laid open to the ever-excessive 'charge' of the cosmic life-energies. At which point, the paradigm of eroticism he is proposing coincides pretty nearly with sacrifice in its pre-Christian and pagan acceptance. The paradigm is human blood sacrifice, driven, Bataille thinks, by a sort of mystical, but still quasi-sexual, ecstasy of breaking and entering, and of fusion with the life-thrust, in all its wild or savage energies of excess.

On the other hand, at the other end of the ethos-spectrum, we have Julia Kristeva, also a twentieth-century French atheist, albeit of a later generation – in her case, the generation of post-1968 Freudian and feminist atheists – yet equally anxious to take back from religion a benefit or good supposedly purloined from humankind by religion or as she says – this is French Enlightenment-speak – 'monotheism'. For Kristeva the post-Enlightenment humanist, the sacred is a form of para-religious white magic (though she does acknowledge the other, blacker, kind, as every psychotherapist surely must). Basically, it's some unexpected epiphany of meaning-and-value in an absurd world: she cites the solemn majesty of British academic graduation ceremonies. (Does Coventry Cathedral know what it is really really doing on those days?) She also cites the iconic, female-vulva, dinner-plate paintings by Judy Chicago (that particular epiphany can be seen, if we dare to or care to, in the Brooklyn Museum of New York).

Registering this diversity of glimpses of the sacred in action, we can perhaps agree provisionally that the sacred is indeed a sort of psychic excitement or electricity, generated and registered within our deepest sensibility, at those points in which we enter into some intimately potent or live contact with external reality (including the nervous and psychic 'internet' linking us instinctively or intuitively to other humans); and that primordial contact with the cosmic life in all things. The immanent sense which we form within ourselves, and carry ever with us, is then available and open to social management; it dances, like the *aurora borealis*, around anything and everything that, as we say, 'turns us on'. It is a 'charge', an 'aura', with which we invest anything and all things 'awesome'. Humankind, on this view, is the sacralising animal; and, in some sense, we answer that definition before we are properly describable as the religious animal – of which more anon, when we come to observe what happens in the first chapters of the book of Genesis.

Once invested, at all events, human sacrality makes the Object invested untouchable – 'sacrosanct', as we say; a talisman promising some wider, perhaps ultimate, communion or intimacy with the mystery of all things. And then we begin to see how the whole group of words organised around the human phenomenon of the sacred comes into play.

Where the reverence due to untouchable or sancrosanct things is defectively observed by others, whether from within or from outside our group, wherever due reverence is actively refused or flouted, we experience desecration, sacrilege. Hence, we may think, the dire extremity of violent punishment visited upon traitors and heretics in the sixteenth and seventeenth centuries. They had desecrated the King's Majesty or they had defiled the sacred bond of sworn allegiance, hence, also, the majesty of the Church, and, indeed, of God's truth itself. This was a crime in the register of sacrilege resonant with, if not exactly identical to, blasphemy. There were no limits to the retribution visited on such offenders. It was terrible and exemplary (hanging, drawing and quartering, the most fearsome tortures, burning at the stake – most of this performed publicly, for the edification of all – and, we notice, for the purging of group intelligence and the remaking of group identity in turbulent times, amid ambiguous loyalties).

From our last example, we can already see that this sacred principle of group cohesion, with its imperative force, capable of overriding all restraint, all relativisation, with its fanatically mobilising energy and its hypnotic corridor of moral blindness, will be a player to be reckoned with when we seek to understand the devastating ferocity and destructiveness of human violence; when we come to take the measure of its perennial nature and omnipresence in human affairs – hence also, of its potential for resurgence in the modern world. To unleash that ever-latent potential, it will be enough to be persuaded that God is 'on our side', hence, that we act in his name – in short, that our very violence, far from being prohibited, restrained or even healed by religion, is, on the contrary, simply and solely sacred.

We will not, it seems likely, be able to get our heads around the tricky notion of the sacred, until we can, at a glance, gather into intelligibility that electric flicker of latent group complicity; until we see that eerie green light dancing over the cause which is projected sacred – making it absolute in righteousness and unhesitating in violence; until we recognise it playing around all the consequent violent acts, making them merciless and terrible. We shall understand the sacred when – to quote, once more, our significantly alerting example – we see it pervading the whole mindset of Islamist *jihad*, coursing through an entire worldview and political strategy, and tracing out those all-too-real shapes of almightiness, apocalypse and terror.

* * *

Which brings us, appropriately enough, to the second dimension of our subject: human violence, in its relation to the sacred. We are already aware obscurely of this link: aware, as I have been busy suggesting, that it is what both fascinates and appalls us in the significantly alerting case of IS. It isn't really that we have never seen any previous avatars of this phenomenon of sacral violence and sacred terror before, in our own culture and civilisation – not if we really think about it. However, the dread epiphany is all the more shocking to us, now, because it rises up in a blindspot of our thinking, in the gap between the expectations of a secularising yesterday and the half-glimpsed eventuality of a suddenly fearsome, archaic-sacral tomorrow.

By way of introducing this theme, I must say something more about where we ourselves stand in our modern violence-threatened and violence-haunted age. A slightly obsessional preoccupation, a fearful fascination with violence, is one of the defining characteristics of the generation of the bi-millennium; and one symptom of this is the number of books that have appeared on this theme in the decade or so either side of the year 2000. I'll characterise briefly just a few of the most interesting keyworks among them, before presenting the thinker – the theology-compatible and believing anthropologist – from whom I borrow my title 'Violence and the Sacred', and who will be our principal guide in these essays.

We live in a residually traumatised age, still processing the memory of the recent world wars, the holocausts, exterminations and genocides of the twentieth century, reputedly 'the most violent century of all time'. This is a problematic age of transition: still under the shadow of a nuclear apocalypse that never quite came to be, but which, equally, has never quite gone away – and which imposes upon us, henceforth, for the first time in history, the burden of knowing that humanity has the power to destroy our planet and put an end to the human adventure as such. We are the tiger envisaged in scenarios of 'mutually assured destruction' (eloquent acronym: MAD).

It's an anxious age, even now becoming conscious of multiple forms of looming, self-generated apocalypse – climate change, the 'clash of civilisations', a potential and very possible Third World War between the 'haves' and the 'have-nots'. Pope Francis has evoked this possibility, developing out of scattered – and at present low-level – local conflicts, so far not yet fused into one. Moreover, we realise uneasily that one form of apocalypse may not exclude the others and that the diverse end-scenarios we fear may, in the event, be combinable and/or cumulative. It is suggestive, at all events, that a considerable number of films have been produced in this time which are variations on the common theme of *Apocalypse Now*.

Such a time, multiply vexed and afflicted by unquiet thoughts about violence, stands in dire need of reassurance. Stephen Pinker, a Harvard psychologist and psychotherapist, sets out to provide it in an 800-page tome entitled robustly *The Better Angels of Our Nature: The Decline in History of Violence and Its Causes* (2011). This is a counterblast to nervous obsession and hysteria; and, at that level, it is an intelligent, useful and fully respectable book; good, for instance, at the naturalist's (Attenborough-type) mapping of the varieties of human violence; and making a serious attempt to plot their distribution in historical time and geographical space, to calculate their relative intensity and destructive force and to retrace the apparent evolution overall of violence in human history.

Pinker's book is significant in reminding us, for example, that the age of the 'hunter-gatherers' was more dangerous, in terms of casualties and fatalities from violence (reckoned proportionately to total population), than is war-weary, murder-ridden, gun-toting modern America. It tells us that the century of World Wars I and II was, on the same basis of accountancy, less terrible and less insecure than the time of Genghis Khan. True enough: most of us have simply no idea of just how blood-soaked and terrifying were the various yesterdays of our species; we lack all reliable perspective on, and all comparative framing of, our own *Sitz im Leben*. Pinker also offers a suggestive first sketch of what changes things. As we might expect, the inventions of civilisation (law and order, the state monopoly of violence – Hobbes' 'Leviathan') do tend to contain violence; just as there are also sources and models of its actual healing or transformation, and, hence, of social and cultural advance driven by spiritual and/or moral and religious progress.

Alas, however, Pinker offers us merely a third-person, cognitivist account of these things. It is not deeply illuminating, not an inside-track story of insightful penetration. Basically, it's a commentary on 500 or so data sets (some splendid, some incomplete, insignificant or downright misleading). These are presented in 500 or so graphs, crunching the statistics. They all retrace the same shape and they tell the same story, which, in point of interpretation, conforms to – but is it not also covertly directed by? – an ideological narrative. All Pinker's interpreted numbers point, in the end, to the same model of positive exemplarity. All would be well – they proclaim – if only all the violent people were more like extremely clever Western liberal intellectuals, of impeccable Enlightenment pedigree, living in the developed world and led by 'the better angels of our nature'. Like the good Harvard Professor himself, perhaps?

Marginalising through aversion all thoughts of the sacred, Pinker may be said to herald another type of reaction to the problem of violence, and one that Christopher Hitchens, for his part, promoted into a proselytising art form. He is here following a path opened up by 'new atheists' Richard Dawkins (the Oxford-based evolutionary biologist, author of *The God Delusion*) and American philosophers Daniel Dennet and Sam Harris. Hitchens' title is explanation enough of this second way: *God Is Not Great: How Religion Poisons Everything* (2007). It is not, clearly, that Hitchens overlooks or ignores the role played in the field of human violence by things religious or archaic-sacral, quite the contrary; he makes a very full engagement with them, but purely and simply – this is the problem – within the perspective of a defining identification which presents 'religion' as the fountainhead of all evil. His book is an indictment, rehearsing – with some slight updating – the litany of accusing derision forged by Voltaire: fanaticism, exclusivist zeal, dogmatic hyper-certainty, authorising all degradations, spawning all cruelties. This devil's brew is laced with the poison of bad faith, self-righteousness and merciless absolutism, and it issues in sectarian rivalries, religious wars, persecutions, torture, inquisition and witch-hunts.

We can see well enough what's 'bugging' Hitchens (and switching on his own sacrally supercharged combativity): the invisible thorn is right there in the amalgam which is practised in his title, i.e. the conflation by sleight-of-hand of different and separate things. In 'God is not Great', we recognise at once the Islamic slogan 'Allahu Akbar', here parodically turned on its head. More than that, and more intimately to the dynamic of polemical indictment, his book returns to sender the defiant 'Die in your rage!' of politically radicalised and violent Islamist fundamentalism. Hitchens' book functions, in fact – though this isn't, of course, an openly declared strategy – by turning an already deviant and extremist image of Islam into the very paradigm of all religions, and of religion as such.

We may readily imagine the impact of this message in the land which is home to *Homeland*, that all-American CIA reality-thriller. Perhaps we recall the episode of the first series in which anti-hero (and turned 'sleeper') Brody rises in the dead of night to purify himself and to begin secret Islamic devotions in his suburban American garage – 'Allahu, Akbar!' Could anything send a deeper shudder of sacred horror through Middle America? Hitchens stokes the fires of sacred horror energetically, the better to '*écraser l'Infâme*' (Voltaire's expression, meaning to crush the infamous-and-unnameable Thing that is perceived to be crawling out of the darkness); and, of course, to sell his book.

I am not – and hope no one is – in the business of forgetting or underestimating those sixteenth- and seventeenth-century horrors of European Christendom but the question is: how can we truly explain, genuinely face, really acknowledge – and actually neutralise them? Who will give us an adequate account of their psycho-social genesis and functioning? An account, distinguishing in full daylight, and to all seeing, between the perverse throwback religious variety, on the one hand, and what we, fondly, but confusedly, call 'orthodox' or 'mainline' religion on the other.

Who will elucidate the interface between the archaic sacred which survives, and sometimes erupts catastrophically, in all of us, and this something else we want to call 'our' religion?

A brief anecdote will give due weight to these questions. In 2007 I found myself in California where Christopher Hitchens – having at that time just acquired American citizenship – was making his promotional tour for the very book I have just been discussing. I caught up with him in the main bookshop of cool and affluent Menlo Park, California. No telly evangelists there. There were only admiring and youthful New Agers, sprinkled with grey-haired Democrat-leaning intellectuals. Hitchens made his pitch, predictably acerbic and audience-pleasing. After which I asked him whether he would take a question 'from an ex-compatriot'. I said: 'Do you know that a few miles south of here, at Stanford University, there is a French professor who recognises very fully all the forms of the "poison" you associate with and identify as "religion"; however, he doesn't call them by that name, but by another, which is "the archaic sacred". And he thinks that the antidote, the answer-in-therapy – hence, the analysis you yourself need and want – lies in . . . well, it lies, actually, in the Christian gospels, which seem, by the bye, to be most strangely excised and missing from your own account of "religion"!'

I explained that René Girard sees a reaction of 'regression', which is latent and possible in all humans, especially in contexts of stress, which trigger fundamentalist reworkings of mainstream religion. These in turn induce a return to archaic behaviour patterns and provide the seedbed in which fully-fledged political ideologies of apocalyptic tenor develop and colonise certain minds, groups and cultures. This is the process we call radicalisation, from which, in turn, actual terrorist vocations emerge. He looked thoughtful and replied, simply – I would even say humbly – 'I would like to read René Girard.'

Up to his recent and untimely death from cancer, I never saw in his writing signs that Hitchens had actually done so. However, I believe there was a perceptible moment when he thought: 'Ah, but wouldn't that be just the sort of theory we most need?'

I am getting around, purposefully, as you will see, to René Girard. Before arriving, however, I must mention a book which provides a very good stepping-stone. It is by an entirely valid interlocutor in his own right. Jonathan Sacks – Lord Sacks, former Chief Rabbi – has quite recently published a book entitled *Not in God's Name: Confronting Religious Violence* (2015). I quote from the jacket blurb: 'Despite predictions of continuing secularisation . . . the twenty-first century has witnessed a surge of religious extremism and violence in the name of God. In this powerful and timely book, Jonathan Sacks explores the roots of violence, focussing on the historic tension between the three Abrahamic faiths: Judaism, Christianity, and Islam.'

Now this is a fine book, as welcome as it is timely. We encounter here a first-rate philosophic mind and a profound theologian. There is great illumination to be had from the way Sacks reads the contemporary context: how he deciphers our present incomprehension of incredulity and horror at IS in the liberal-democratic and secularised West; or the violence which has erupted, in interestingly similar patterns, within each of the Abrahamic monotheisms; or the interrelations between them, which he explicates, tellingly, in terms of a sibling rivalry, played out within the fields of theology and identity politics. His re-readings of the common core Abrahamic texts are interesting and hopeful. All of which offers another understanding and make for better, more reconciled, more brotherly relations, transcending violence and war.

These things make Sacks a natural interlocutor for the present Girardian readings of the same realities, pursued over an, at least, partially, overlapping course, and this dialogue has a propitious beginning: Sacks has actually read Girard. He even borrows two key perspectives of his theory: mimetism, which is, for Girard, the driver of supercharged and sacralised violence; and scapegoat theory, which is in Girard the paradigm of sacred violence in operation. He sees the Shoah (Holocaust) as the central and paradigmatic case of this, as does Girard, save that Girard still places centre-stage the Passion of Christ, paradigmatic expression and once-and-for-all-time exposure of the functioning of sacred violence and the victimary mechanism. However, these are, as we shall come to see, two views, through different ends of the same telescope, of very much the same phenomenon.

Thus, saving up for future chapters some of the riches of Sacks' book, we come to René Girard. He died, aged 91, at the beginning of November 2015, passing away peacefully, at his home just off the campus at Stanford University, California. A few words of introduction are called for at this point, if those who know little or nothing of him are to follow the unfolding patterns of his thought. They are very aptly provided by tributes appearing the day following his death in the French Catholic Daily, *La Croix* (5 November 2015). Not everything in them will be transparent as yet but my concern, at this stage, is simply to establish the pertinence of Girard for our title themes:

> René Girard, violence unmasked . . . René Girard, decipherer of the Sacred . . . He devoted his work to the analysis of human rivalry and violence and saw in Christianity the transcending of these things, the way beyond them. . . . Girard identifies the place where the sacred emerges, in the practice of sacrifice, in that form of sacrifice in which the scapegoat is sacralised, divinised. He [the scapegoat] will henceforth carry the vocation of preserving the reconciled community; sacrifical ritual allowing humankind to reactivate the social bond, and myth permitting us to preserve the memory of it'.

We take due note: violence, the sacred and, even, towards reconciliation. Can we perhaps already tease out certain implications of his theory?

> This Violence and this Sacred are, for René Girard, the origin of culture. Humanity is born out of the religious dimension of things ['l'humanité est fille du religieux']. . . . That's why Girard says: we live in sacrificial societies, i.e. societies in which the inner logic of primitive sacrifice, if not its outward forms, is still observably at work.

Which means, among other things, that 'we are always convinced the Other is guilty': 'One day the new, unheard-of word arrives, with Christianity, telling us that victims are not guilty. This revelation deconstructs all cultures.'

How, then, are we to see René Girard's achievement and significance?

> He built an intellectual infra-structure, a platform for intelligent thinking, which is indispensable to any non-violent enterprise. . . . He re-introduces the Old and New Testaments into the bloodstream of secular thinking. . . . He quoted Simone Weil: 'The Gospels, before becoming theology, that is to say a science of God, are anthropology, which is to say: a science of man.'

Finally, 'René Girard: controversial Christian thinker and a warm-hearted man of "immense intellectual holiness".[2]

I will try to elucidate and amplify that very bare outline in chapters to come, drawing occasionally on the important books which have begun to appear on Girard the religious thinker and fundamental anthropologist. The second chapter will take us through mimetic theory, in which is embedded René Girard's understanding of violence and the sacred. The third will explore his master-concept of the 'founding murder'. The fourth will engage with his writings on the Old and New Testaments. The fifth will move from Passion and Resurrection to reconciliation. The concluding sixth chapter is the ground-sketch for a Girardian-inspired strategy of reconciliation.

* * *

Already, however, we have something of a vantage point. We have seen how the mysterious and ill-understood notion of the sacred might be some sort of pointer to the origin and nature of violence, and to the moral ambiguity of human nature, whether anthropologically or theologically deciphered. We can begin to see, at least in principle, how the sacred might provide Hitchens with an understanding of his 'poison'; and Sacks with a formula for his elusive common ground between the Abrahamic faiths.

We may conclude this first chapter with two quick GPS location-fixes, designed to retrace and to verify the vantage point reached after this first foray into a complex topic and to trace out some of the new steps to come. Both GPS readings present themselves in the form of myths (one ancient, one modern).

GPS location-fix number one. The common frame of understanding of violence, common at least to the Abrahamic faiths, and accessible also to others, is provided in the Bible by the story of creation, temptation and fall given in the opening chapters of Genesis: that profound and seminal account of shadow upon splendour. The splendour, as French philosopher Paul Ricœur has brilliantly shown (in his *Penser la Bible* [1998] – 'Thinking the Bible'), is the cry of jubilation and praise that rises up in the earliest humanity, re-echoing, exultantly, out of the deepest ontological sensibility of the human creature in contact with the world: order from chaos, the provision of all things needful in a

---

2. This last quotation is taken from the single tribute I know to have appeared in the British press: Michael Kirwan's tribute in *The Tablet*, 14 November 2015.

garden of delights; the joys of language, the otherness of gender, of human fellowship, sexuality, language. That is, ontologically speaking, the first dimension within which the animal-become-human is, upon psychic awakening, addressed by the Creator; and that joyous electricity of praise leaps from summit to summit within a bonded Eden.

However, that bonded sphere of communion with the world and its Creator admits of a secret presence and a 'lining' of dark otherness, a black sacrality. If not ultimate, this insinuating presence is at least ancient, intimate and fascinating, and it is animal in nature; today, we should say, it is continuous with man's own animal antecedence in evolutionary time. That other, darkly sacral voice insinuates the urge to rival the Creator, so as to realise an autonomous and self-sacralising divinity: 'Ye shall be as gods, knowing good and evil' (Genesis 3:5). Exactly so: that godlike 'shot' or 'thrill', that ersatz transcendence, is the definition of what Girard understands by the sacred. 'Gods' – that plural stands, surely, in memory of the polytheism Israel too has known and, yet, the text gives us 'as gods', in recognition of delusory or mirific character of the travestied godlikeness thus realised, and its status as caricatural inversion of the reality it would imitate.

At once, that darker principle is seen to be expressed in violence, with the murder of Abel by Cain, the elder son of the first couple. Human violence spreads a corrupting disorder: it contaminates civilisations, it infects nature. The darkly self-sacralising animal is the super-violent animal. Enough to make the Lord God all but repent of his creation. The tribal god of Israel is still, for the moment, the 'Lord of Hosts', mighty in battle, very much a 'God on our side'. If we revisit the narratives of the conquest of the Promised Land and the internecine struggles of Israel's sacral Kings, they contain tales of divinely inspired ethnic cleansing, revenge and massacre, with distinct prefigurations of IS; narratives, all of them, of the Iron Age, which, by the bye, coincides pretty nearly with the creative but very violent period that runs from ancient Israel's beginnings (early second millennium BCE), as traced in the Hebrew Bible, through to the rise of Islam – roughly, from 1,500 BCE through to 700 CE. The Covenant and the Law provide the necessary bonding and binding of the people of faith: 'I have set before you life and death, blessings and curses. Choose life, so that you and your descendants may live' (Deuteronomy 30:19).

One hopes that anthropology and theology, secularist and believer, and all Abrahamic theologians among themselves, might agree to agree, after negotiation, each party in their own way, about that common

What Is 'Sacred Violence'?

framing of the problem which we have to face in common. That would be a helpful first step of common understanding, setting us on the road to a common praxis of reconciliation.

GPS location-fix number two comes in the form of a modern parable, brilliantly developed in the novel, then film, *The Life of Pi*. An Indian boy, forced to emigrate with his family from their native land, is shipwrecked in a violent storm mid-Pacific on the way to Canada. He takes to a lifeboat, in company with a variety of animals escaped from a zoo, which the ocean-traversing and shipwrecked freighter had been carrying in its hold, including a magnificent and fearsome Bengal tiger (yes, the tiger puts in a return appearance!). A splendid and terrible adventure of survival on the great ocean of life ensues, in the perilous company of this magnificent Beast.

At one point, the survivors' lives are saved by a sojourn on a floating island of vegetation, composed of mango-tree roots. It is inhabited by a whole marooned population of bright, inquisitive little meerkat-like creatures, dashing about everywhere, chattering interminably, and threatening to out-populate their exiguous living space. Rather, one feels, like humanity, on our teeming and ever more globalised (westernised?) little planet. The meerkats, of course, pay their tribute to the predation of the tiger and they crowd anxiously around strange sinkholes in the vegetation, which appear to communicate, way down below the floating tangle of twisted roots, with the great ocean depths. In daylight, the Indian boy swims with delight in the transparency of these pools, reflecting only the sky, but at night these same pools become fearsome, secreting an unknown acid or poison which is discovered to have dissolved entirely the corpse of a previously shipwrecked Survivor and so the boy must take again to his tiger-carrying lifeboat and drift on, east-west (and East to West).

In Canada, we are offered two narratives by way of decipherment: there's a pragmatic, utilitarian and superficial one, as demanded by the owners and the insurers of the lost freighter. To please them, the boy survivor listlessly agrees to rewrite his tale, so that humans alone now fill up the entire frame. This imposed narrative returns him, in effect, to the anthropocentric, secular and uprooted floating island, from which he has just escaped, with its deadly secret of ultimate uninhabitability.

According to this account of things, his companions on the ship and in the lifeboat were really only ever crew-members: the hyena-like cook and the zebra-like sailor; and and as to the tiger, Why, was that not just the violence within the boy himself? Yet, that moral allegory of rivalry, conflict and violence between men captures almost nothing of how it really was; and it serves only to deny the wondrous variety, richness and colour of human experience, and its depth in evolutionary time, together with those very stories about violence told by the world religions, Hinduism, Judaeo-Christianity and Islam. (The Indian boy is specifically seen in the film to have inherited from all those sources.) All have prepared him to survive, despite the accompanying tiger, on the great cosmic ocean of the mysterious blue planet and all are preferable, in the end, to a dessicated wisdom which desacralises the cosmos exactly to the extent that it secularises human culture.

We're not told what the right interpretation is. This is a reflexive, postmodern parable, respectful of those contemporary values: multicultural plurality, inclusiveness, relativism, non-closure. The hermeneutics are explicitly left to the film's writer-figure, who is tasked with establishing the to-be-published version of the story (and who, of course, represents us, the audience of the parable).

At least we can see that the parable reflects in mythic wise, and that it reflects upon, our fast-globalising, multicultural world. We can also consider the fundamental enigma of those sinkholes which communicate with our own depths in evolutionary time and which engage our own survival in a world of splendour, a world, however, that is haunted and overshadowed by violence – cosmic, animal and human.

We see how vast and ramified is the problem we have begun to tackle under the name of the sacred, as well as its protean forms and its fundamental ambiguity. Perhaps, too, however, we have a sense of how the chances of decryption rise, as we admit that the sacred is linked aboriginally to human violence and as we attend with ever-sharpening focus to the meaning and nature of 'religion'.

That's where we are at the end of this first chapter; and it's pretty much where we all are in the wider scheme of things. In the next chapter we join Girard himself for some more sinkhole diving, as we try to unravel further those tangled and ancient roots of the enigma of violence and the sacred.

2
Violent Origins, Origins of Violence

Both the myths just referenced in Chapter 1 are, in some sense, myths of violent origins. They problematise – and, in part, they already answer – the strategic and crucial question: 'Where does violence come from?' 'What are its origins and causes?'

Genesis replies: it's a form of ersatz sacrality, a form of false or idolatrous transcendence; it originates in a violence of spirit born of man's misconceived attempt to imitate and outdo the creator God. It's a form, and, certainly, it's a symptom and a sign, of the constitutional human exile from true harmony with God (the exile or estrangement known in Christian theological tradition as original sin); and it's a pointer to the disasters of murder, and of cultural and cosmic disorder, that immediately, in the book of Genesis, illustrate the meaning of that exile.

The other, postmodern, myth, the one which has still to be written up in book-form, replies: Violence? – that'll be the beast we wake up next to, right there in the lifeboat beside us; it's the tiger in ourselves and other animals and in the cosmic forces of nature around us; it's the beautiful and dangerous beast which, on anybody's account, shares with us our fragile human attempt at salvation – leastways, at survival – adrift, as we all are, on the cosmic ocean of sentient life, in this vast and enigmatic cosmos.

The Life of Pi is, specifically, a post-Darwinian myth: human violence is discovered first of all through its roots in animal violence, which in turn seems to be derived from violence discerned in the primordial forces of cosmic nature. (In the film that is the fire that destroys the floating zoo and the devastating ocean storm, which initiates the adventure of shipwreck and lifeboat-survival.) We remember those sinkholes we noticed as crucial features of the uprooted miniature island refuge floating somewhere in mid-Pacific. They communicate still with the primordial ocean depths; they are shafts of insight and profundity, reaching down, in daylight, towards mysteries of origin. At least, they have that value as far as the onward-travelling boy is concerned; even if they no longer perform that function for the mass of marooned, secular meerkats, who cluster chattering around the sinkholes, but never jump in.

The time has come for us to jump in and to dive down. I'll try to do some sinkhole exploring, as it were, and to see what we can see of the ocean depths, in the expert company of evolutionary submariner and fundamental anthropologist René Girard. He is the modern theorist who does most, I feel, to answer the aspiration present in both myths to 'mind the gap': the gap of spiritual exile in Genesis; the gap of postmodern uprootedness, of fragmented coherence and fractured wholeness in *The Life of Pi*. Girard, I will suggest, shows us how to get the problem of sacred violence into sharp and strategic focus, thus enabling us to come most profoundly to grips with the tiger.

Two chapters will be needed in establishing this case. First, I'll say something by way of introducing mimetic theory: the theory in which is embedded René Girard's whole approach to violence and the sacred. That will point us towards the interaction of violence and the sacred which we should expect to find at the threshold of our becoming human.

I will come then, in the next chapter, to the 'original scene' Girard envisages: the basic model scenario of 'founding murder' which his theory posits. That will help us see how this Girardian model of origins offers to unlock the still very little understood enigma of hominisation and the beginnings of human culture and civilisation.

Taken together, these moves will open the account of what I have called the foundational complicity between violence and the sacred; and, it will, I hope, equip us to turn around, in all senses, the problem of sacred violence, still extant today.

**

Mimetic theory is so called because it refers centrally to the notion of mimesis – the Greek word for imitation. It was Aristotle, very early in human thought, who glimpsed from afar that what distinguishes humankind from animals is not so much our superior skills and higher faculties; it is, rather, the faculty of imitation we share. He didn't fully grasp the reach or fully develop the potential of that idea. He could not do so, because he had no notion that the human species actually does stand in line of evolutionary descent from animals; and he was prisoner of a limiting idea – to which our own thinking is also mortgaged – namely, that imitation is a relatively second-rate sort of asset: that it is, as we often say, *mere* imitation. (We can see how that idea arises: Aristotle is thinking of mimicry, parody etc., those particular forms of imitation which can indeed appear more derivative and secondary.)

However, look at the very different way Girard himself develops the same notion of imitation. Imagine, he says, a three- or four-year-old child introduced into a room rather like Hamley's toystore, filled with gorgeous toys of all shapes and sizes; within which there is, already installed, another child, who is already playing with an already chosen toy. Which toy, then, in this whole fairy-palace of toys, will the new child desire to play with?

Without thinking, we all know the answer to that question: he will want precisely the toy the other child is already playing with. Why is that? The reason is that he is attuned, immediately and fundamentally, to reading the desire of the other child; so that the first child's preference, to which the second child 'locks on', becomes the highlighted model for his own preference. He wants, most determinedly, what the other child wants; and so he is imitating, not just this latter's externally visible gestures, behaviour (etc.), but also his inward and entirely invisible desire; he's reproducing the other child's estimate of value ('Wow, great toy!') and his intentional goal ('I must have it').

In human beings, there is an amazing and profoundly defining aptitude for immediate group understanding, founded on mimesis. We are built by evolution to represent, empathise with, replicate and reciprocate any and all forms of stimulus, behaviour or attitude; we copy-in-reciprocity (I hold out my hand, you hold out yours) and what we read and decipher first of all is one another's desire. That is what makes us the most social, the most highly collaborative species in nature, which is, more than anything else, the secret of our evolutionary 'success' as a species.

Mimesis creates the very possibility of human reciprocities, of human relationalities of whatever kind. What is the first thing a newborn child does – apart, that is, from the things other animals also do (like suckling, excreting, sleeping, crying etc.)? We all know the answer to that question too but how many of us have actually stopped to realise how wondrously novel and prodigiously significant it is? The mother *smiles*, her child *smiles back*. Research on the neurobiology of imitation has shown how this reaction is produced: by the firing of what are now called mirror neurons in the frontal cortex. That is the first characteristically human response; and, we may notice, it is something much more immediate and basic than a learned reaction or a rational, calculating one.

It is something akin, perhaps, to group electricity in pre-human animals, to the instinctive mirroring which allows huge shoals of fish, for instance, to flicker and turn, as one, in unison, so as to confuse predators, and which allows the octopus or squid to change colour to match the seabed onto which it subsides; or the lyre bird to mimic any and every bird in the Australian forest. It is this faculty of mimesis that enables the higher primates to evolve the most basic systems of communication, to interiorise learned models of behaviour (such as tool use in crows or in chimps) and to respect certain proto-cultural norms (like dominance patterns). 'You little monkey', we say to our children, when they infuriate or delight us by replicating adult tricks, expressions or manners.

However, we also now know something that bypassed Aristotle: namely, that animals are, in point of fact, not that good at imitation, whereas human imitation is immeasurably more sophisticated and developed, diverse and insistent, and, above all, more freighted with consequence, than is the case in even our nearest pre-human evolutionary relatives.

Animals – that is to say, pre-human animals – do imitate each other, certainly: in learning certain basic skills; in reproducing basic group emotions like hostility or fear; or in basic behaviour like the 'fight or flight' instinct. When they fight their own kind, however, full mimesis – mutually other-imitating reciprocity – barely comes into it; there is no supervolting 'tit-for-tat'. They are contending merely for what they need in order to survive – territory, mates, food etc. This means that animals of the same species fight to the death only very rarely (it does happen, but it's an accident, an exception).

Human imitation is altogether more intimate and complicated. We enter imaginatively into the inner world of other humans. We desire things because we see someone else desiring them. We are, elementarily, interested in their interest. That 'turns us on', as we say, and makes those things desirable to us. What is fashion but novelty made desirable and imitated? What is advertising except the proposing and manipulation of models of desire? What is a market, except a place of exchange subject to judgements of desirability, which are then copied: 'New York sneezes and London catches cold'. Mimesis all! 'Do you copy that, Red Leader?' Yes, of course he does; we all do when we learn anything at all or communicate anything whatever. We interiorise and replicate inwardly the message or the meaning or the model in the very process of taking it in, making it ours and the human world would fall apart if we didn't (cf. Girard, *TH* 1987: 17).

A large spectrum of the latest research in human neurobiology, in developmental and group psychology is currently confirming, in spectacular ways, the unsuspected range and significance of the phenomenon that largely bypassed Aristotle. Leading French neuropsychiatrist and animal behaviourist, Boris Cyrulnik, in the best and most recent overview currently available of the brand-new and galloping science of imitation studies, writes: 'Western thought is organised around a misconceived centre-point: the individual. . . . It is imitation that organises the biology of our being-together, the affective glue that allows us to receive and respond to Other-pressure, which is what tutors our becomings' (Cyrulnik 2018: 3).

For this leading scientist, imitation is a hugely positive thing: we imitate to bond and to learn and to become, by affiliation and by cultural development, more than we already are. Girard, for his part, recognises perfectly well what he calls 'positive mimesis' but his distinctive contribution in this field is to develop the unsuspected and hugely important darker corollary (or shadow side) of this same phenomenon – 'negative mimesis'. Yes, he perceives, we copy other people's desire. However, that immediately means: two hands reaching out in rivalry for the same object and, very soon, coming into conflict; becoming progressively mimetic in their very rivalry; engaging in retaliatory 'tit-for-tat' (as we call it); and, in that process, mobilising the entire psychic energy and resource of each antagonist; even to the point of sacrificing life itself (witness: the suicide bomber); and, on the way or subsequently, mobilising also, in a mimetic chain reaction, the energies of all our allies and all their allies (witness: the mimetic fascination of the *jihad*). To understand in Girardian terms this latter phenomenon, we simply have to factor in that further multiplier of mimetic effect supplied by the peculiar conditions of internet communication; and no doubt, also, some traditional factors of identity politics, such as the assertiveness and paranoia of displaced and alienated minorities; and, of course, not forgetting the peculiarly electrifying effect, produced within an Islamic culture-sphere, of the declaration of the Caliphate. (What we are currently observing, as I write this in 2019, is that the recruitment of foreign *jihadis* has declined sharply since that supreme authority, the Caliphate, with its claim to absolute archaic-sacral obedience, has been lost, along with its territorial basis.)

The dynamic of mimetic rivalry is, in other words, built in from the beginning to the mimetic potential of human groups. This is the unobserved factor which any adequate reading of the geo-political context within which IS has arisen and developed will also have to come to grips with. Hence the interest of understanding mimesis thoroughly: the better we analyse the making of that driving force, the better equipped we are to deconstruct and dismantle it.

A further point that will reward careful attention is this: mimetic fascination always locks us into that rivalry, that conflict. Rivalry itself, having become mirror-like and fascinating, can take us over entirely, with a dynamic all of its own, which is obscurely compelling, to the extent, we have said, of leading some to deliberately sacrifice their own lives to the sacred cause. That spectacular symptom of mimetic rivalry alerts us to something more general still, which is that we forget the limited stake for which we had begun to contend and to fight in the first place. What takes over in the end – but it has been implicitly present from the beginning – is always, Girard insists, metaphysical: the pure assertion of our own identity-in-being, rivalling with – and threatened by – some other-identity. That hidden cause and origin is, by definition, sacred (i.e. untouchable, non-negotiable), at least within the first 'natural' framing context, as provided by evolutionary process, with its master-imperative of survival.

Moreover, there is another consequence. In mimetic violence, antagonists who began by wanting merely to assert their own distinctive identity become monstrous doubles of each other; strange twins, as it were, locked together in identical retaliatory acts of verbal, imaginary and then actual physical violence; becoming indistinguishable from each other, as the sacred violence of metaphysical self-assertion takes over each and makes each the 'spitting image' (as we so revealingly say) of the other. (This is the passage from 'appropriative' mimesis to 'agonistic' or 'antagonistic' mimesis.) Already, in Girard's very first work on desire in the European novel, this negative electricity of conflictual 'undifferentiation' (i.e. the progressive loss of difference) sparks and crackles with negative psychic electricity (*DDN* 1961).

That same book presents us with the Girardian 'triangle' of mimetic desire, designed to map out the relationship of the Subject of desire, with its Object and with the mediating/adversary Other. What this structural figure most fundamentally shows is that the relationship described is not inert or stable. As rivalry mobilises all energies, in individual or in collective subjects, the triangle begins to spin wildly, uncontrollably, on its axes in various planes and to morph, as it does so, into various forms of black hole. These are capable of decisively warping social space, just as black holes in the cosmos distort and violently transform physical space.

To this basic structure of negative reciprocity – mutually Other-imitating rivalry – Girard adds, that is to say, an account of its dynamic quality. The conflictual charge of mimetic rivalry in humans will tend to increase exponentially; and it will become contagious externally, catching up and drawing in third parties precisely because it engages, throughout the whole social field, reciprocal mimesis – that great and unseen multiplier or 'turbo' of desire.

In the end, what we are being asked by René Girard to grasp overall is something truly momentous: there is an unsuspected runaway dynamic at work in human affairs. Those black holes of violence – represented by feud, vendetta or crusade – will tend, fatefully, to deepen, proliferate and fuse; thus drawing into conflict and thence into violence all relationalities within a given community. Something of this fundamental dynamic – albeit in a strictly limited (still, for the moment, inhibited, relatively 'civilised' and mainly non-violent) form was evident in the polarisation of the debate in this country over Brexit.

That secret dynamic is worth thinking about both in relation to humanity's violent past and, even now, in relation to our fast globalising world and the more 'apocalyptic' perils of our todays and tomorrows. What, for instance, do we most fear about *jihad*? Surely, that it will generate a logic of generalised conflict, sucking in, on the one hand, those Western societies which have developed out of mediaeval Christendom and, on the other, all members of the worldwide Islamic community: that is the nightmare of 'the clash of civilisations' – and it is not yet yesterday's nightmare. Is it not, precisely, the strategy of IS to provoke just that generalised and apocalyptic paroxysm, to 'bring it on'?

Once we learn to decipher the mimetic nature of desire, once we see the rivalry and conflict it engenders, once we measure its power of contagion and its supercharging drive towards paroxysmal outcomes, it will be apparent that any human grouping, local or worldwide, is subject, visibly or invisibly, to an extreme peril of violent implosion (from internal conflict) or explosion (from the clash of external antagonisms). From which it also follows (in all deductive rigour) that containing and managing self-generated human violence must be the prime enabling condition and the number one imperative of human social life at all times and in all places. (When MPs and media pundits remind each other, as they so frequently do, that 'ensuring the security of our citizens' or 'defending our nation against attack' constitute the 'prime function of government', they are, obscurely, registering and enacting this fundamental anthropological reality.)

Here is a radically new and disturbing light on what anthropologists are accustomed to calling 'group intelligence' in humans: it represents the obverse face of human superiority in nature, as gifted to us by evolution. Here is the peril that answers human potential – its apocalyptic shadow side. That's why we're worried and, if we know ourselves and our species adequately, that is what we should worry about.

* * *

The exact path that leads Girard from these general, but fundamental, insights and perspectives of mimetic theory to his precise scenario of original founding murder cannot – there is not 'world enough and time' – be examined here.[1] It's a detective trail: a path of hypothesising, modelling and confirmation that passes though the study of Greek tragedy, through the anthropology of primitive religions and of world mythologies. It includes: an intense encounter with English and American anthropologists, Frazer, Malinowski, Radcliffe Brown, Robertson Smith and others; and an even more close-up and personal struggle with those fathers of modern deconstructionism, Freud and Nietzsche, whom Girard sees as having glimpsed – but mis-deciphered and malappropriated – the figure of human origins to which he is increasingly drawn. However, we do not need to retrace that same path minutely in order to gain a vivid, imaginative glimpse of the scenario

---

1. The best consolidated account of the Girardian hypothesis of origins is to be found in 'Book 1 – Fundamental Anthropology' of *Things Hidden*. The way of discovery leading there is best mirrored in the first eight chapters of *The Scapegoat*; perhaps, indeed, in this sentence of conclusion: 'The foregoing analyses oblige us to conclude that human culture is condemned to a perpetual dissimulation of its own origins in collective violence' (Girard, S 1986:100).

of origin which René Girard envisages increasingly in the development of his anthropological thinking. It appears – and Girard himself acknowledges the prescience of this precursor sketch – in the climactic scene of William Golding's novel of 1954, *Lord of the Flies*.

This novel, it will be recalled, is set in the era of an imagined nuclear war. A group of British Anglican choirboys – surely, the most 'innocent' representatives of civilised humanity? – is being evacuated to Australia. On the way, they are – by interception or in the after-shock of a nuclear blast - brought down and crash-land on a Pacific island. They attempt to reconstruct the orderly, liberal and decent way of civilised living they have left behind. However, everything begins to fall apart, as they revert to primitive patterns traced out by the 'hunters' (led by Jack). Piggy, the enlightened rational thinker of the group is killed. Ralph, the responsible democratic leader, is hunted. Simon, the – perhaps Jewish – prophet, discovers that the feared and hated 'Beast', said to inhabit the forest, is no more than the decomposing corpse of a dead pilot, gruesomely suspended from the forest canopy by his parachute – he's been shot down in the larger conflict that rages above and beyond the island.

The climactic scene of sacred violence is set against the background of a fearsome electric storm.

> 'Going to be a storm', said Ralph, 'and you'll have rain like when we dropped here. Who's clever now? Where are your shelters? What are you going to do about that?'
>
> The hunters were looking uneasily at the sky, flinching from the stroke of the drops. A wave of restlessness set the boys swaying and moving aimlessly. The flickering light became brighter and the blows of the thunder were only just bearable. The littluns began to run about screaming. . . .
>
> Jack leapt onto the sand. 'Do our dance! Come on! Dance!'
>
> He ran stumbling through the thick sand to the open space of rock beyond the fire.
>
> Between the flashes of lightning the air was dark and terrible; and the boys followed him, clamorously. Roger became the pig, grunting and charging at Jack, who side-stepped. The hunters took their spears, the cooks took spits, and the rest clubs of firewood. A circling movement developed and a chant. While Roger mimed the terror of the pig, the littluns ran and jumped on the outside of the circle. Piggy and Ralph, under the threat of

the sky, found themselves eager to take a place in this demented but partially secure society. They were glad to touch the brown backs of the fence that hemmed in the terror and made it governable.

'Kill the beast! Cut his throat! Spill his blood!'

The movement became regular while the chant lost its first superficial excitement. And began to beat like a steady pulse. Roger ceased to be a pig and became a hunter, so that the centre of the ring yawned emptily. Some of the littluns started a ring on their own; and the complementary circles went round and round as though repetition would achieve safety of itself. There was the throb and stamp of a single organism. The dark sky was shattered by a blue-white scar. An instant later the noise was on them like the blow of a gigantic whip. The chant rose a tone in agony.

'Kill the beast! Cut his throat! Spill his blood!'

Now out of the terror rose another desire, thick urgent blind.

'Kill the beast! Cut his throat! Spill his blood!'

Again, the blue-white scar jagged above them and the sulphurous explosion beat down. The littluns screamed and blundered about, fleeing from the edge of the forest, and one of them broke the ring of the biguns in his terror. . . .

'Him', 'Him!'

The circle became a horseshoe. A thing was crawling out of the forest. It came darkly, uncertainly. The shrill screaming that rose before the beast was like a pain. The beast stumbled into the horseshoe.

'Kill the beast! Cut his throat! Spill his blood!'

The blue-white scar was constant, the noise unendurable. Simon was crying out something about a dead man on a hill.

'Kill the beast! Cut his throat! Spill his blood! Do him in!'

The sticks fell and the mouth of the new circle crunched and screamed. The beast was on its knees in the centre, its arms folded over its face. It was crying out against the abominable noise something about a body on a hill. The beast struggled forward, broke the ring, and fell over the steep edge of the rock onto the sand by the water. At once the crowd surged after it, poured down the rock, leapt on to the beast, screamed, struck, bit, tore. There were no words and no movements but the tearing of teeth and claws.

> Then the clouds opened and let down the rain like a waterfall. . . . Presently the heap broke up and figures staggered away. Only the beast lay still, a few yards from the sea. Even in the rain, they could see how small a beast it was; and already, its blood was staining the sand.
>
> Now a great wind blew the rain sideways. . . . On the mountain top the parachute filled and moved; the figure slid, rose to its feet, spun, swayed down through a vastness of wet air and trod with ungainly feet the tops of the high trees; falling and still falling and the boys rushed screaming into the darkness. The parachute took the figure forward, furrowing the lagoon, and bumped it over the reef and out to sea,
>
> Towards midnight the rain ceased and the clouds drifted away, so that the sky was scattered once more with the incredible lamps of stars. . . . Along the shoreward edge of the shallows the advancing clearness was full of strange moonbeam-bodied creatures with fiery eyes. . . . The water rose further and dressed Simon's coarse hair with brightness. . . . Somewhere over the darkened curve of the world the sun and the moon were pulling. . . . Softly, surrounded by a fringe of inquisitive bright creatures, Simon's dead body moved out towards the open sea.

What is Golding suggesting to us? Fundamentally, that violence is an evolutionary legacy and a reversion to primitive patterns programmed into us by our evolutionary past.

We can see this if we look at the behaviour to which the 'hunters' regress. The hunters, yes. By reason of evolutionary provenance, man is a carnivore, hence also a violent predator. Evolutionary biologists tell us meat-eating is, precisely, associated with the growth spurt involved in that emergence which we call hominisation – the larger, more complex human brain required the richest proteins; animal predation, in which homo sapiens shares, assures our survival; more than that, it underlies our higher development and flourishing. Multiply that antecedence of predation with the 'turbo' of mimetic and rivalrous desire, that peculiarly human phenomenon which, with Girard's help, we are just beginning to discover, together with its contagious and incremental dynamics, and one begins to see why humans are 'superviolent' – why we are nature's ultimate tigers.

Now look at the hunting dance. This is a form of mimetic group behaviour with, precisely, a runaway dynamic of crescendo towards paroxysm. Normally, for our hunter-gatherer ancestors, the hunting dance would mimic the animal tracked: here, the pig actually hunted and killed. The animal, in such tribal rituals, is conjured up, in order to mobilise the hunters' own power over it, in anticipation of the hunt. However, the dance called for in this case (by Jack: the leader of the hunters become 'lord of the dance') is a variant form of that standard ritual. It is performed (by all of his tribe) to ward off everything they fear, not just the hunted animal, but also the darkness, all the whole awesome power of cosmic nature, the baleful will of the heavens over them ('the threat of the sky') and that larger, unnameable dread which they project onto their adversary, 'the Beast'.

We can see Golding's point. This is a form of exorcism and/or propitiation – those are the words we need to understand archaic religion, most especially, where it involves blood sacrifice: exorcism of that awesome dread; propitiation of the cosmic violence of the storm (Golding's text stresses the 'whip' of those lightning flashes, the 'blows' of thunder); propitiating, actually and in fact, the supposed author of those whip blows. Yes, because without knowing it, the terrified boys are projecting into the heavens a 'monstrous double', an adversary Other born out of their own inner violence and torment.

This dance is undertaken, as we see clearly, to process and manage their own obscure collective distress; its effect will be to cook up and distil, by mimetic contagion, their sense of the sacred. They enter into a self-induced frenzy or trance generating the most basic feelings of unanimity and group-power: through music (chanting, rhythm) and movement (circling, stamping). And the ritual becomes, in its climax, a form of runaway violence. Golding then shows us a mob beating or lynching of the adversary who, eerily, materialises out of the darkness and stumbles into their citadel (or circle); the circle that is also compared, tellingly, to a mouth, complete with a 'tearing of teeth and claws'. The boys collectively have become – and, as the crescendo of the dance reaches its sacrificial apex, they actually are – the Beast, i.e. the Other they most fear.

We can see how that dancing circle forms a 'demented but partially secure society'; how the boys are protected by 'the fence that hemmed in the terror and made it governable'. However, highlighted too is the way in which their trance, and its violence, are cognitively and morally blind: in their frenzy, they kill without knowing it – not an animal, or a malign spirit – but a fellow schoolboy who appears where they expect 'the Beast' to appear, out of the forest darkness ('Him', 'Him'). We have all heard of wish-fulfilment; this is dread-fulfilment. It is nameless, inarticulate, undeciphered – and so self-fulfilling – dread.

What Girardian things should we take from this scene? Human violence is, at bottom, a mimetic phenomenon, a fascinated and fearful mirroring of the Other. It is originally and always, somewhere deep down, sacred violence (despite its apparently 'casual' and merely 'expedient' or 'instrumental' later developments and forms, which we recognise more easily, since that is what our culture expects to find). Yet, still today, human violence is sacralising in at least two important senses. First of all, negatively it demonises its Other but then it is also positively 'self-sacralising' (positively speaking, it divinises itself). Always, it is sacrificial, requiring a victim; and, originally and in principle, that sacrifice is bloody.

It is also dynamic and that dynamism, marshalling all psychic resources, is obscurely sexual. It rises to a climax, which must have orgasmic relief in killing, in the spilling of blood. Violence is violation: we speak – how revealingly! – about 'blood lust' and we recognise its presence in the sex orgies and in the child sacrifice which feature in primitive religions, including, in the Bible, the rites practised among the Canaanite tribes surrounding Israel.

We notice, finally, the self-mystification involved in this scene of originary violence; and the irony it generates. Simon has come, precisely, to deliver the hunters from the superstitious dread that haunts them – and they kill him. They themselves exhibit the truth that the transcendent and baleful adversary they fear is, in fact, a 'monstrous double' of themselves, because they themselves 'project' heavenwards their own collective violence. In the language of Luke's gospel: 'They know not what they do' (Luke 23:34). That's a word about human self-misrecognition in general but, most especially, and quite crucially, it concerns human violence, pointing then also to a grievous and harmful self-mystification – and, ultimately, to a human misrecognition of God.

Perhaps we begin to see the pattern of Christian allusions in this passage? Who is killed? Simon, the – Jewish? – prophet; Simon, the deliverer (a Messiah figure, therefore); Simon, the scapegoat victim of a collective lynching: yes, this is a sort of crucifixion, meant to recall 'the dead man on a hill', who is made to pay for that blind frenzy which requires its victim, its blood-sacrifice. Simon is then also, we note, 'recognised' by the cosmos: there is a 'poetic' kind of endorsement, as the universe reclaims its own, its emissary victim, its prophet, its Messiah.

This is, of course, a muted or diminished echo of the Gospel theme of Resurrection. It is muted, diminished or elided for reasons that bear a moment's reflection, since they may well belong as much to ourselves, as to Golding or to his theme. Perhaps Golding does not believe in that element of the Christian story, while yet seeing its extraordinary pertinence. Perhaps he believes that 1950s Britain does not believe it any more? Perhaps he feels that his countrymen should be left nevertheless to chew on that striking and suddenly challenging pertinence.

We may refine further this play of speculative insight. Perhaps the favoured theories of atonement known to Golding in his postwar 1950s, amid what one academic has recently called 'The strange decline of Protestant Britain'[2] (dating back to that very decade), remind him too painfully of a fully natural or archaic religion. Perhaps he wants to show that this island 'tribe' has slipped back, precisely, to a stage of human development before and below the threshold of Christian revelation.

Perhaps, correspondingly, he mutes this theme for the most simple reason of all, which might be that, pre-dating René Girard, Golding never had the occasion to understand simply and clearly how the 'sacrifice of the Cross' is a replay of humanity's 'original scene' – albeit, a replay that changes everything.

At all events, we can say without any speculation, that Golding gives us, acknowledged by Girard, a deeply pertinent sketch of the sacred violence of human origins (if not – not yet – an insight into the strangely productive resolution of that drama to be found in the Gospels).

So now, what, specifically, is Girard's own scenario of founding murder?

---

2. Inaugural lecture of the Rt Rev Professor Ian Bradley at the University of St Andrews, 1 May 2018. This lecture is currently available and may be consulted on the University website. https://www.st-andrews.ac.uk/staff/teaching/teacherstalk/inaugurallectures/2017-2018/. Date of access: 7 December, 2019.

3
Girardian 'Founding Murder'

What does René Girard mean by 'founding murder'? The expression itself is taken over from Freud, who provided in *Totem and Taboo* the first sketch of a 'scientific myth' of human beginnings.[1] This represented the murder of the imagined father of Darwin's 'primitive horde' as *the* founding event: that is, the single and unique occurrence at the origin of the first human community from which all else flowed.

For Girard, however, Freud's psychology is visibly modelled on the fables of Greek mythology after which his 'complexes' are named. He borrows these structures of psychic complication from the mythical heavens and re-projects them, first, into the psychic 'unconscious' and, from there, onto the data of archaic pre-history. Yet Freudian psychology, though it resonates with the deeper and darker places of the troubled human myth-making imagination, is cognitively impotent. Even as it signposts the overriding significance of desire-led strife and violence in human affairs, and even when it points to a principle of founding murder, that mytho-poetic co-resonance with human pre-history does not, in any reliable sense, describe or explain what actually happened at the threshold of hominisation. Too much myth, not enough science.

The Freudian intuition, nevertheless, allowed Girard to see 'sacrifice' as a commemoration and to explain its contradictory aspect: an act of violence that was transgressive and criminal, on the one hand,

---

1. Founding murder is a key concept which runs throughout Girard's work: at first, implicitly, then more explicitly and fully theorised, with ongoing revisions. See *S*: 88-99; *TH*: 24-25, 96-7, 124 and 105-25 ('Myth: The Invisibility of the Founding Murder'). The implicit beginnings of the concept are best followed in *VS*: 92, 210-18; and in 'Mimesis and Violence',(1996: 9-19).

but purifying and legitimate, on the other. It put him on the track of a single solution bringing together the origin of the gods and the origins of human societies. It also led him to declare the idea of a single originating event of parricide inadmissible scientifically, since it presupposed everything it was designed to explain: family, prohibition of incest, rivalry with the father – in fact, Freud's Oedipus complex.

Girard, for his part, reworks the archetypal Freudian myth in the light of his intense engagement with the best ethnological and ethological discoveries of the twentieth century, now interpreted and combined according to the powerful new insights of mimetic theory. What he discovers is that that founding murder is the art of 'violence contained' – contained, that is, by a selective, exemplary and therapeutic dose of violence (rather as, in medicine, antidotes are derived, pharmacologically speaking, from poisons) – and that this art, inaugurating archaic-sacral religion and cultural invention, made 'civilisation' possible.

In his revised version, the scenario of founding murder is not so much an event, as a structural reduction or paradigm of the complex processes and relationships which, over many thousands of years, allowed the process of 'hominisation' to clear a decisive threshold of survival, self-regulation and self-fashioning progress realised within organised and viable societies.

Girard distinguishes, fruitfully, two steps or phases which Golding conflates and Freud never imagines: on the one hand, a spontaneous original lynching or scapegoat murder, putting a provisional end to the crises of intra-community violence; and, on the other, its ongoing, institutionalised – and therefore truly founding – ritual repetition in the form of human blood-sacrifice.

At the threshold of hominisation (i.e. the point of evolution when the species *homo sapiens* becomes fully formed biologically and all but stabilised in that definition), a characteristic scenario must regularly have been played out. We should not fail to notice the word 'regularly': this is not any sort of one-off; it is a scenario played out, with variations and developments, perhaps over tens, even hundreds, of thousands of years.

The community undergoes a paroxysm of violence (the 'mimetic crisis', 'the 'sacrificial crisis'). This is defused *in extremis* by a self-organising mechanism (the 'victimage mechanism') which inaugurated, historically speaking, and still, residually, secretly, undergirds all social life and everything we call culture. It constitutes, in natural process, the emergence of culturally active, self-fashioning humanity. Girard's careful discernment of this emergence leads him to a precise, coherent and developed account, susceptible in principle of empirical verification, of how the victimage mechanism functions so as to open up this space of human potential and its development in culture.

Where the adversaries within a conflicted social group or community originally wanted diverse things – to appropriate the same woman, to seize food or territory or power, to exact retributive justice etc. – they end up polarised, quite irrationally, upon a single adversary, arbitrarily designated to the common fury by a single rage-modelling leader. In other words, each gathering crisis of generalised violence tends to simplify, at its apex, into a polarised and unanimous antagonism of the type 'all-against-one'. The collective blood-rage is, at this point, deflected outwards and discharged against a single, arbitrarily chosen – and, consequently, quite innocent – victim. The crisis is resolved, for the time being, by a scapegoat murder.

The scapegoat acts *de facto* as a sort of lightning conductor to all the violently destructive energies gathered within the community. The mechanism of emissary victimisation declared here may be compared to the disconnector switch that breaks the circuit and prevents the perilous electricity of mimetic and rivalrous desire from consuming the human house. It also sets up the first equation of collective identity bonding: a very disturbing equation, albeit strangely familiar to us from the long echoes of resonance it finds in all periods and places of human history. All are one, against and by virtue of, the rejected, demonised and scapegoated adversary Other.

Then something quite remarkable happens. Girard asks us to imagine the victim lying inert before the hushed group of hominids or primitive men. He/she appears simultaneously and contradictorily as: (i) the *guilty origin of the crisis* – he/she must have been guilty or we wouldn't have killed him/her, nor would we have peace through his/her death; and (ii) as the *beneficent provider* of the miracle of renewed peace and social harmony. (Girard does not hesitate to speak here of 'reconciliation' [TH 1987: 102]; albeit in the full knowledge that this is 'reconciliation' in a provisional, precarious and primitive form.)

This moment of conflicting persuasions and surpassing awe is the beginning of a process of sacralisation: the dead victim will come to be seen as the potent bearer of a power of life and death, and then as the power capable of reversing the current of life-energies from negative to positive; such terrible wrath, such amazing beneficence! Here is a new type of collective attention, centred on the victim, henceforth become the generative matrix of a new process of 'transcendental' signification, the focus of a new dimension of meaning-making. (*TH* 1987: 99).[2]

The first perception will suggest in retrospect, as it comes to be deciphered collectively, that the sacrificial victim must surely have willed his/her own death; the second, once the corpse has been disposed of, will come to suggest that this exceptional and departed visitor must indeed have been a divinity in disguise.

The sacred, in other words, is generated by violence misrepresented, misinterpreted, mythically hypostasised (*TH* 1987: 42). Myth itself, considered in its generating point of origin, is a falsified account of the victimary process, tending to conceal the real guilt of the sacrificers, while transferring blame, implicitly and illegitimately, to the victim and convincing the community that this episode of crisis was a blessing in disguise, hence, also, a legitimate sacred action brought about by the god himself (*TH* 1987: 148). The erstwhile victim becomes then the attributed divine origin of all the prohibitions and rituals instituted to prevent a recurrence of the same crisis.

This scenario gives us the origin and meaning of sacrifice in its archaic-sacral first form:

> The word 'sacrifice' – sacri-fice – means making sacred, producing the sacred. What sacrifices the victim is the blow delivered by the sacrificer, the violence that kills this victim, annihilating it and placing it above everything else by making it in some sense immortal. Sacrifice takes place when sacred violence takes charge of the victim; it is the death that produces life, just as life produces death, in the uninterrupted cycle of eternal recurrence common to all the great theological views that are grafted upon sacrificial practices – those that do not acknowledge the demystifying effect of the Judaeo-Christian tradition. It is not by chance that Western philosophy begins, and

---

2. This expression marks a key recognition-point in the relation of Girard's theory to the linguistics-inspired, formalist anthropology of Lévi-Strauss. R.G. is asked (*TH* 1987: 102-3): 'Are you referring to the idea of a transcendental signifier which has been energetically rejected by current thought?' He replies: 'I am not saying that we have found the *true* transcendental signifier. So far, we have only discovered what functions in that capacity for human beings.' The victim for Girard is, in human practice, the operative signifier, the buried centre from which irradiates all human signification. He leaves unsaid, to be explored, the possibility that, as declared in the gospels, the true signifier is Christ.

up to a certain point ends, in the intuition of eternal recurrence that the pre-Socratics and Nietzsche hold in common. This is the sacrificial intuition par excellence. (*TH* 1987: 226)

The original spontaneous murder is already *implicitly* a sacrifice: a scapegoat victim is, unwittingly, but in sober fact, done to death that the community may not perish. However, it is not yet a sacrifice in the classic sense we are used to from the practice and discourse of organised religions. It is only incipiently and by chance an act of communion, assembling the community around the victim-god; it is not yet a deliberate and concerted act of violent expulsion and ritual murder.

We know with an ever-increasing weight of evidence that ritual human blood sacrifice features prominently in the pre-history and early civilisational history of all ancient cultures: from the Aztecs to the Celts, from the peoples of the Mediterranean to the tribes and religious communities of India and China. It is also widely acknowledged that sacrifice – in a thousand varieties and developing forms – was the most original and constitutive practice of all world religions.

What, however, functionally speaking, is sacrifice?

It is, says Girard, with breathtaking simplicity, at the heart of the common life a re-enactment or replay of the originally spontaneous and unreflecting first murder. Why replay the trauma of a collective murder? Because, in processing that spontaneous collective lynching that has mysteriously saved the community from self-destruction, the conviction becomes established that the episode was indeed sacred and should indeed, by ritual repetitition, be declared, confirmed and broadcast as such.

The ritual slaughter of a surrogate victim consecrates this memory totemically. It repeats the salvational spell and makes it binding, at the lowest possible economic cost to the community – this single victim will stand in for the community, will become its emissary in calling down the god, taking the hit and procuring the god's renewed blessing on the community. Thus, it replicates as exactly as possible – here is an intuitively brilliant leap of Girardian hermeneutical imagination – a re-enactment or restaging of the original scapegoat murder, driven by the *arrière-pensée* of recreating its cathartic, reconciling, identity-bonding outcome.

The victim is chosen, often from a purpose-specific reserve (as in the case of the Aztecs and many other known cases), from among the marginal, the weak or the vulnerable (e.g. children, the sick, the handicapped, prisoners of war). This rite is triggered by the incipient signs of returning mimetic crisis; these are actually laid out – they are prepared and, indeed, solicited – by the institution of 'carnival', which significantly frames the sacrifice. The sacrificial climax of the festival – here is a further brilliant intuition of Girardian hermeneutics – 'exorcises' and 'resolves' once more this staged renascence of violent contagion and conflict within the social group, but this time ritually, which is to say, repeatably.

Girard's account of the logic of 'carnival' explains why, in all primitive cultures, institutional practices, such as funerals, marriages, hunting, animal rearing, rites of passage and so forth, characteristically bear the structural imprint of the mimetic crisis and end with an act of sacrifice (*TH* 1987: 48-79). He concludes: 'At first it may seem unthinkable that all human institutions could arise from a practice as seemingly negative and destructive as sacrifice . . . but, finally, the number of victims is small, whereas prior to sacrificing them, there is licence to replay the [mimetic] crisis, that is to say to engage with any number of partners in all the sexual, alimentary and funeral activities which are normally prohibited within the group' (*TH* 1987:78-79).

The collective, strongly participatory and essentially theatrical character of the rite comes to be ceremonially regulated and aesthetically enhanced over time – delivering a, no doubt, spell-binding potency of emotional charge. We have a good idea of this from the much later homologies of theme and the affective echoes it finds in Greek tragedy, which develops precisely out of this archaic-sacral religious ritual. (Girard here elucidates, in principle, and then, in rigorous, detailed exegesis of the great works of Sophocles and Aeschylus and Euripides, the 'birth of tragedy', i.e. the goal more polemically and mythically sought by Nietzsche.)

At the threshold of hominisation, Girard tells us, such inventions rationalised and refined – as they still do today and still, in a more or less operative sense, mythically – the same underlying logic of the violent control of violence by symbolic and ritual means. That logic remains 'underlying' because the true nature of the forces in play is hidden from the operating subjects or agents. Girard speaks powerfully, here in dialogue with the alternative 'formalist' modern theory of myth which he finds and rejects in Lévi-Strauss, of 'the invisibility of the Founding Murder' (*TH* 1987: 105-20).

Violence is 'contained', yes – but at a cost. The act of founding murder limits the contagion of violence; it cuts short its overt ascendency within the community. Yet, at the same time, the practice of emissary violence is secretly interiorised within the group. It is diffused throughout the whole sphere of its systems, works and ways; and the more effectively so, because that founding act is articulated and officialised in the form of a tribal mythology which covers up its own violent role in the victimary-sacrificial process. A complicity with violence thus becomes recycled, normalised, naturalised. We are in violence and of it before we know anything about it. If 'scapegoat' means 'innocent constrained to take the hit for others', we will never spontaneously, of our own seeing, notice as such any scapegoats that 'we' ourselves make, only ever the scapegoats made by other tribes, other agents, human or divine. We are thus constrained by, even contained within, the violence which we have 'contained'.

At that price, the victimary mechanism is, as Girard shows, an ever more fruitful generative principle, building up culturally and institutionally the communities organised around it. That centrepiece of founding murder, re-enacted and memorialised in the rite of blood sacrifice, ensured the conditions of collective co-existence needful to an emergent humankind: security, social stability, the bonded complicity required by collaborative actions.

* * *

Talk about 'things hidden'! We shall be talking about those hidden things for the next three chapters but one of the greatest of them requires some foundational attention immediately. This is the strange fact that we don't know how *homo sapiens* came to emerge as a species (see *TH* 1987: 88-89). In continuity with the animal world? Assuredly; but also, increasingly, caught in a quantum leap of distinction and difference, through the development of what we call culture, which is simply – on this account – a hyper-developed, codified, generationally transmitted and renewed programming of group intelligence.

Girard believes the victimage mechanism and the archaic-sacral religion developing from it allow us to decipher the logic of invention of the 'software' programming the psychic space we collectively inhabit – to reconstruct, that is, the inventive logic at work in that world-changing emergence, inflecting the course of evolution as such: the advent, of human culture.

He makes good this claim by systematically taking us through the ways in which that cryptic but crucial victimage mechanism provides the trigger, the focus and the opportunity required for the further development of the principal vectors of culture: symbolicity and language, first of all; then, the earliest prohibitions; leading over time, to the moral codes, laws and institutions which enabled societies to function by controlling their objects of desire and, therefore, also the risk of conflictual mimesis; then, the development of more complex sacrificial rites and structures, guaranteeing a binding cohesion internally, enabling greater social hierarchy and extending political control and operative also, externally, in managing Other-relations, both for the avoidance of risk, for the keeping of the peace and the acquisition of commercial advantage. Some inventions, like prohibitions (interdicts, taboos), develop a first logic present in the victimage mechanism, the need to limit, prevent and avoid violent conflict; others, like ritual sacrifice, from the second, equally potent, logic present within it: that of developing its transfiguring benefit or blessing of peace, unity and collaboration.

Reading René Girard, we grasp a suddenly evident and deeply sobering fact: that the entire panoply of cultural invention engendering 'civilised societies', including moral codes, religions, laws, social and political institutions and practices, is – at least originally and elementarily (that qualification is, clearly, a very weighty one) – derived from primitive ritual practice, including, most centrally, ritual blood sacrifice.

Finally, expressing both logics mentioned above, come the mythic stories which are bonding in an identitarian sense and are often, indeed, stories of real historical foundation, albeit falsified so as to edit out the truth of an actually-and-in-fact founding murder. Thus, the myth of Romulus and his brother Remus is the story of the fratricide which founded Rome; albeit rewritten to edit out all blame attaching to the founder of the city (*TH* 1987: 146).

As Girard shows in an impressive range of examples taken from different cultures and parts of the world, these mythic identity narratives are unfailingly told in a way which edits out, or covers up, with a sort of artful artlessness, 'our' own participation in founding murder. Thus humankind survives its own violence, thanks to an organising principle of symbolico-ritual sacrifice, while, at the same time, protecting its own self-image and safeguarding its energies of self-belief, enterprise, dominance (and other forms of Darwinian advantage) with buckets of auto-administered and self-deceiving whitewash (known in Girardian parlance as *méconnaissance* or 'misrecognition'). The species negotiates in this way the 'double bind' of the Darwinian struggle to survive and, in particular, the perilous ambiguity of the call to a super-tiger status in nature, its constraints becoming in the process a resource and a developmental springboard.

Meanwhile, the possession of this hermeneutical key enables René Girard to decipher in turn the functional logic of the principal components of the entire system of primitive religion-and-culture – in other words, the most fundamental factors or vectors of identity bonding. We have named them and not one is missing: shared prohibition (taboo, interdict), shared ritual (in particular, ritual sacrifice), shared moral codes, laws, institutions, political practices. It is in this sense that Girard quotes approvingly, in an interview of 2009,[3] Lucien Scubla's view of his work claiming that this same key has enabled him to unlock all the 'stalled decipherments' of Victorian anthropology.

His basic model of human origins is 'foundational', then, in the primary sense that it permits and enables inaugurally the entire process of culture-driven hominisation that follows from it: the invention of cultural practices, of developing social order, of moral and religious progress, of civilisational advance. It founds what humanity has become and the very possibility of its becoming through mind-made means, through culture.

* * *

Are these hidden things important? We might try thinking about that question in the following way. When contemporary anthropologists of human origins pick up the telling of the evolutionary tale, it is observable that they are, in general, deeply reluctant to give the peril of human violence any nodal or originary place in their scenarios of origin (*TH* 1987: 88). The only struggle (or *jihad*) they imagine, when confronting the problem of human origins, is with the environment and with deficient technologies. They are apt to think, following Rousseau, of human culture as based on a social contract hammered out rationally between consenting and even – implicitly (this assumption is never stated and remains invisible to its proponents) – *modern* adults. The chances of that scenario being true, are, in Girard's submission, close to zero.

He sees this reticence as one more confirmatory sign of an aboriginal blind-spot of human self-awareness and even as a symptom of the very syndrome his theory is concerned to elucidate. He speaks of 'our tenacious desire to ignore violence and its generative power, until the very end, when it thrusts itself upon us', and, in the same breath, he

---

3. See 'From Animal to Human', reproduced in the Appendix to the present volume, p. 123.

speaks of our 'immemorial inability to decipher it' (*TH* 1987: 123). There is, Girard is suggesting, a *deep-seated aversion* which is declared when we are confronted with any such model of origins which makes human violence a mainspring, a source or a foundation; because it jogs us, disturbingly, with the suggestion that the hidden mainspring may still be a live, pivotal and generative force in our own world. Such reactions are imprinted with what psychiatrists call denial: the (usually) unconscious suppression of a painful emotion or truth. Girard tends to read them as an evolutionary residue within the individual and/or collective psyche of the logic of archaic-sacral mythologies, in which – as we have come to understand thanks to Girard – all recognition of the scapegoat victim, of the victimary mechanism as such, and, especially, of the moral agency and responsibility of the sacrificers, is 'radically eliminated' (*TH* 1987: 105).

Yet the pertinence of the Girardian model of violent human origins is acute. If, on the one hand, it constitutes a modelling hypothesis which many modern minds reject *a priori*, it is also, contrariwise, the sort of reading we ought to anticipate and predict and explore with greatest care – if Darwin's theory of the descent of man is broadly correct.

Darwin's theory presents nature itself as a super-sacrificial self-organising system. Yet it really leaves *homo sapiens* out of the picture, except in respect of his his descent from animals. If we wish to integrate humankind as such into Darwin's big picture, it will be necessary, structurally speaking, to graft onto his theory a model addressing the novelty of man and explaining how a new type of self-organisation comes into play and fundamentally changes the evolutionary deal or game. It will have to explain: (i) how mimetically turbo-charged humans 'made it', in the first place, across a performance threshold at which their very superiority threatened to wipe out the species *homo sapiens* as such; (ii) by what mechanisms – and/or what magic – these perils could be disarmed, and those violent energies re-channelled into new possibilities of cultural invention and self-management; and (iii) the generative logic by which the principal elements of organised archaic-sacral culture came into being, thus providing the ongoing matrix within which human culture, human specificity, could develop in self-fashioning mode. Girard's account of founding murder does, *con brio*, those three requisite things.

In doing so, it goes a good way towards relieving the general ignorance which Girard diagnoses in natural scientists and philosophers about the process of hominisation: 'We have absolutely no idea what early cultural practices consist of, how they interlock with "natural" processes, and how they act on the latter to create more and more humanized forms' (*TH* 1987: 88).

Tempting as it might be, we cannot dwell here on Girard's very suggestive account of the way human intelligence grafts its developmental inventions onto proto-cultural forms already present in animal species. It is clear enough that the categories ethologists are concerned with are also very much those involved in Girardian founding murder: rival fights, mobbing, redirected activity, victimary and transferred aggression, appeasement ceremonies; triumph rites – and so on. Discussing the role of 'functional change' in evolution, the Austrian naturalist Conrad Lorenz even describes behaviour patterns which, if we did not know their animal context, might be innocently read as describing Girardian founding murder in humans:

> However, all these amazing metamorphoses seem tame in comparison with the ingenious feat of transforming, by the comparatively simple means of redirection and ritualization, a behaviour pattern which, not only in its prototype, but in its present form, is partly motivated by aggression into a means of appeasement and further into a love ceremony which forms a strong tie between those who participate in it. This means neither more nor less than transforming the mutually repelling effect of aggression into its opposite.
> (Lorenz: 2002 [1966, 1963]: 168)

We might wish to compare this with Girard's own reflection in *Things Hidden:* 'Animal rites of this kind provide us with everything necessary for an understanding of the transition, based on sacrificial religion from animal sociality to human sociality. We need only postulate a greater mimetic intensity and the resulting rivalry that would trigger the actual victimary mechanism foreshadowed in the animal rites' *(TH* 1987: 98*).*

Girard's late-flowering reflection on human origins leads him, at all events, to major conclusions that provide the hinge articulating animal nature and human culture. This new articulation or 'bridge' may be expressed clearly, if summarily, in five successive pointers given in *Things Hidden*:

> There is reason to believe that the power and intensity of imitation increase with the volume of the brain along the entire

line that leads to *homo sapiens*... It must have been the increasing power of imitation that initiated the process of hominization, rather than the reverse, even if this process subsequently served to accelerate that growth and made a prodigious contribution to the remarkable power of the human brain.
(*TH* 1987: 94-5)

Beyond a certain threshold of mimetic power, animal societies become impossible. This threshold corresponds to the appearance of the victimage mechanism and would thus be the threshold of hominization. [. . .] What has been missing so far is a model for the organizing and driving factor in the process, a motor for this strange machine. The victimage process gives us this motor.
(*TH* 1987: 95-6)

One can understand how the primate in process of hominization, this hypersexual animal armed with stones, always disposed to hunting and war, could have transformed the extreme threat of self-destruction that hung over him in the crucial phases of his biological and cultural evolution into a force for cultural development.
(*TH* 1987: 96)

There will always be simultaneous rupture and continuity between all social forms, from animal to pre-human, and finally to human. The problematic nature of mimesis and the victimage mechanism allows us to understand that there will always be social forms based on imitation, even among animals, and that these forms must collapse in mimetic crises before they can generate new and more complex forms based on the surrogate victim. Between what can strictly be termed animal nature on the one hand and developing humanity on the other there is a true rupture, which is a collective murder, and it alone is capable of providing for kinds of organisation, no matter how embryonic, based on prohibition and ritual. It is therefore possible to inscribe the genesis of human culture in nature and to relate it to a natural mechanism without depriving culture of what of what is specifically, exclusively, human.
(*TH* 1987: 97)

> In the founding mechanism reconciliation is achieved against and around the victim. [...] Because of the victim, in so far as it seems to emerge for the community and the community seems to emerge from it, for the first time there can be something like an inside and an outside, a before and an after, a community and the sacred. We have already noted that the victim appears to be simultaneously good and evil, peaceable and violent, a life that brings death and a death that guarantees life. Every possible significant element seems to have its outline in the sacred and at the same time be transcended by it. In this sense the victim does seem to constitute a universal signifier.
> (*TH* 1987: 102)

We see how the human animal enters the symbolic order, and therefore the domain of language; how he begins to create meanings beyond what mere physical gestures can signify.

More usefully still, Girard's scenario of founding murder enables us to understand what appears at first sight to be a considerable, perhaps even an insurmountable, paradox. How is it, in a post-Darwinian evolutionary perspective, that archaic-sacral religion turns out to be the new matrix of human cultural and societal invention, the real instructress ('*institutrice*') of our pre-historic ancestors and the fundamental crucible of developing human specificity?

Humanity as such is 'born out of the religious dimension of things' (*BE* 2010: ix). If natural first-form religion is seen as the aboriginally containing force and the functioning magic spell that checks, converts and re-channels the destructive energies of the competitive struggle for life as observed by Darwin, then that paradox, though it bids fair to rearrange a number of cherished pieces of our mental furniture, may well be on its way towards a very healthy and cogent resolution.

* * *

All well and good, we might think, but can we rely on Girard's hypothesis? We can, if we are prepared to remember maturely its epistemological status and what that implies. Girard's account of the still little understood process of human emergence remains, of course, a *hypothesis*. It is a theory, subject in principle to various types and degrees of confirmation (and disconfirmation) by many empirical sciences. This dialogue of confirmation and disconfirmation, however, should not be imagined, naively, as a simply achieved reality check. Girard offers a big-picture retrospective decipherment, reading back from more complex, advanced or evolved stages of culture to the discernment of its origins and threshold emergence; and this is in many ways an inverse form of hermeneutic to that practised by the natural and, even, to a lesser extent, the human sciences.

The effort of natural scientists is directed to reconstructing the process of human emergence by retracing its actual footprints in time, by passing from lesser to more complex realities and by working towards an integrated overall picture. However, few would deny – though it may surprise us to observe how few people actively imagine it – that, an approach to the problem of hominisation from both ends of the problem (temporally and epistemologically understood) is desirable and that a complementary partnership, between different disciplines of thought and between empirical enquiry and theory-led hypothesising, is in principle possible.

In the present case, considerable areas of overlap, commonality and convergence have indeed already become apparent. They are reviewed in the second Darwin-Girard volume, *How We Became Human* (Antonello and Gifford 2015b: xi-xlvii). The extent of such confirmatory echoes, convergences and exchanges to date may surprise sceptics, perhaps even persuade them that this is indeed a very serious scientific theory. At the very least, the attention expended on examining this question will tend to discourage the type of immediate high-minded denial (usually philosophic or theological) that comes, simplistically, from construing founding murder as though it were a tabloid headline: '*Missing Person H. Sapiens. GRISLY DISCOVERY OF "FOUNDING MURDER"!!!*'.

More specifically, the coming together of theory-led and empirical approaches to questions of the beginnings and emergence of human culture and civilisation has been and is being pursued very fruitfully: in the field of archeological excavation of the oldest known sites of central and S.E Turkey. Ian Hodder, Director of excavation and Dunlevie Professor in the Department Archeology at Stanford University, who knew Girard personally, writes of this collaboration in the recently published book which he edits: *Violence the Sacred in the Ancient Near East. Girardian Conversations at Çatalhöyük* (2019).

Hodder speaks of two realms of endeavour suddenly and contingently brought together thanks to the accident whereby archaeologists committed to the old perspective of Neolithic societies dominated by notions of fertility and the mother goddesses, found themselves having to come to terms with evidence provided by imagery of wild and dangerous, often male, animals, often set in confrontation, together with traces of ritualised violence, such as the teasing and baiting of the adversary animals confronted in hunting. This need for explanation bumped into a theory of sacred violence in search of concrete examples: 'Because [Girardian] theory links ritual violence to social order, it seems ideally suited to explain the evidence from sites such as Göbekli Tepe and Çatalhöyük. Could the killing of wild bulls at Çatalhöyük be seen as a re-enactment of the killing of the sacrificial victim?' (Hodder: 2019: 4). He reports Girard as responding in complementary fashion: 'I believe that these paintings and the whole of the Çatalhöyük settlement are an enormous discovery from the point of view of the mimetic theory' (2019:4). [4]

Hodder concludes: 'Indeed there is much potential for bringing the Neolithic archeology of the Middle East into conversation with Girardian theories, so long as a critical stance is maintained. (Hodder, 2019: 4). The *caveat* is predictable and necessary: it relates to the normal exigencies of evidence-based empirical enquiry; and to the inevitably different focus and persuasion of theory, related to its power of coherent sense-making and explanation. The encounter of these two perspectives, he says, presented some 'problems': are we required to think *homo erectus* had no culture? Do hunters really sacrifice animals? Why do rituals that link violence and the sacred have to derive from an original event; and why does that original event have to be a human sacrifice? Is Girard's hypothesis too 'Christian' to be taken seriously? (Girardians may tend to think all of these 'problems' amenable to further elucidation and/or to greater familiarity with the theory!) (Hodder, 2019: 4).

On the other hand, the acknowledgment by Ian Hodder of cogent new light brought to bear on the archaeological data by Girardian theory is impressive. 'Scapegoating and mimetic theories are attractive not only for Çatalhöyük and the origins of settled life in the Neolithic of the Middle East, but also for archaeological theory more generally' (Hodder 2019: 10). 'Mimetic theory provides a startlingly fresh perspective on several taken-for-granted building blocks of archaeological theory and method' (Hodder 2019: 23). This 'productive new perspective', he suggests, gives an alternative view of cultural transmission ('imitation' is re-interpreted and now takes account of no longer deniable phenomena of collective

---

4. Girard's own commentary on the animal baiting drawings from Anatolia is published in Antonello and Gifford 2015b, Antonello and Gifford, 215b: 262-288

violence).⁵ An alternative to the approaches of Cognitive and Evolutionary Psychology is provided (allowing a new flexibility of thought and real progress on old issues such as: when did humans become religious?; were humans always cooperative or were they originally violent?). Finally, the Girardian approach provides a quite invaluable generative mechanism explaining how cultural invention works. 'Perhaps the greatest attraction of the Girardian view is that it provides a strongly generative account in which religion, symbols and culture are emergent properties of the mimetic process' (Hodder 2019: 17).

In view of this fruitful type of interaction between empirical science and Girardian theory, the most profitable question for the undecided who wish to take a serious option on the value and indeed, the eventual 'truth' of the Girardian scenario of origins, is perhaps this: why would our first human ancestors *not* have sacralised obscurely, in dreamlike unknowing, the very self-organising mechanism of social regulation that appeared to convert their greatest human peril into a life-opening source of seemingly unlimited, quasi-divine human possibility?

If the key fits the lock, if it turns without too much fuss, if it actually opens that first door, and then others, and others still, the chances of Girard's theory of the origins of culture becoming, like Darwin's theory before it, substantially vindicated after much lapidatory doubt, will be getting better. As we come to understand that point, we shall be better placed to understand not just the specificity of humankind in Darwin's evolutionary tree of life, but where the book of Genesis itself, written many thousands of years later, is coming from, and how and why it is revelatory and a new departure.

From this account of the primary sense of 'founding murder,' we should expect to encounter a larger and looser secondary sense. This expression describes not only the probable scenario of our actual threshold emergence to cultural development and human specificity, but now, by extension, a logic of collective attitudes and behaviour which is ever-latent and very widely resurgent in cultural forms extant today. Founding murder, in that case, describes an evolutionary legacy transmitted from this first or originary practice which pre-programmed and enabled our own coming-to-be as a species.

Speaking of the effects of 'misrecognition' with Italian philosopher Gianni Vattimo, Girard suggests that early religious mythologies are not the only ones to perpetuate a transfiguring alienation of the

---

5. Hodder refers to 'a long chronology of violence among 'hominins' (Allen 2014, 21), stretching back at least 5 million years.

violent human subject. They find themselves in good company with philosophy, psychology, ethnology and all the human sciences, which are all, to this extent, open to the charge of being so many 'modern mythologies' (Girard and Vattimo 2009: 146).

Indeed, the victimage mechanism, with its weird and wonderful logic of violence contained, sacralised, monumentalised in ritual practice and so transformed, with canny unknowing, into a formula for survival and flourishing, is so central to the coming-to-be of humankind, so creatively and continually generative, that it will always provide a perspective of approach, analysis and interpretation capable of elucidating almost any human phenomenon at any moment of history.

Any sector of cultural activity (exemplified at random, e.g. literary criticism, economic practice and theory, the thought of Freud or Nietzsche), any culturally embedded attitudes and behaviours (at random, anorexia, the policy of nuclear deterrence, megachurch attendance) will declare to the gaze of the practised mimetic theorist a hidden desire field, displaying mimetic patterns and structures. Also, the more fully formed, accurate and subtly comprehensive the theorist's reading of that field, the more it will declare the point, the pattern and the logic of founding murder.

Needless to say, the more remote in time and space from the original model is the phenomenon explored, the more the exercise of exploring it will require historical and contextual awareness, together with guarantees of coherence and rigour, and some tried and tested good sense, preferably of an interdisciplinary background and character.

This secondary sense calls for two comments. One is made by Girard, when he remarks that his theory is not a school of thought, but 'a concrete proposal for studying and better understanding human reality' (Barberi 2001:26). The other is that we *are* as we have, in evolutionary process and in cultural emergence, *come to be* – just as the Bible's first book, in its very title (Genesis), reminds us.

* * *

Interesting stuff, some of us may still be thinking. Nevertheless, in the last analysis, this whole scenario of founding murder is ultimately pure logico-deductive speculation, isn't it? Lively imagination, maybe even sheer fiction – just like Golding! Where is the fieldwork, the evidence?[6]

---

6. The not uncommon notion that Girard is unconcerned with empirical research is a confusion of mind: the fundamental anthropologist is by definition

Please look at this. Here, courtesy of *National Geographic*, is an artist's reconstruction of the world's oldest known temple, discovered and under excavation (for the past fifteen years or so), at Göbekli Tepe in south-east Turkey, on the road 'out of Africa'.[7]

It is very old indeed, dating from more than eleven and a half millennia ago (c. 9,600 BCE), just after the end of the last Ice Age – a staggering 7,000 years before the Great Pyramid of Giza and more than 6,000 years before our own Stonehenge.

The entire phenomenon is surprising and subversive of long-cherished ideas. It seems well-nigh incredible, to begin with, that a monument of this size, ambition and degree of sophistication could have been constructed by multiple roaming bands of hunter-gatherers, united only in the task of that construction and to the end of the rituals performed here. That shock alone has been compared to coming across a jumbo jet, entirely constructed with household tools, in a suburban garage.

The very confident dating it has been possible to make, and the incontestable religious function of the structure, are just as astounding and even more deeply subversive of received ideas. It used to be thought, by Victorian anthropologists and their twentieth-century epigons, that ancient religion was one of the things – like writing, effective weapons and commerce – that flowed from settlement and civilisation. Somewhere between domesticating animals and putting a man on the moon, human beings 'invented religion' (cf. *TH* 1987: 66-75). Not so: that precise dating, that irrefutable function of archaic-sacral cultic worship have sufficed to prove conclusively that religion precedes settlement and they suggested to the first director of excavations, the late Karl Schmidt, that religion is indeed the matrix and the impetus of the entire cultural and civilisational development that followed – exactly as envisaged by Girard, following and adapting the founder of modern sociology, Émile Durkheim.

Something else is arresting and deeply suggestive. The prodigious quantities of arrowheads, spear-points and flint knives found at the site prove beyond question that this temple was also, among other functions and attributes, some manner of 'weapons factory'. It associated, naturally and inescapably, violence and the sacred.

---

conducting a second order reflection, in which he engages most strenuously with all the relevant empirical research-based evidence. This engagement can be quickly verified in e.g. *VS* and *TH*. For an interesting example of dialogue with and alongside fieldwork specialists, see the case discussed in the present chapter and detailed in Hodder (2019).

7. See Charles Mann, 'The Birth of Religion', *National Geographic*, June 2011: 34-59.

How exactly? If we knew that, it would help with another, related question which we can resolve only by surmise and deduction: what sacred rituals went on there? How did they arise out of hunting and cultic offerings? What was the earliest archaic-sacral 'worship' actually like?

There are clues in the design of this temple. In part, it reminds us of a liturgical amphitheatre, heralding the simpler, more classical lines of the amphitheatres of Greek tragedy. It is thought that the common spectators gathered round on the earthen banks, built up against the outside walls of the enclosed space, and looked in from the outside on the cultic ceremonial within; while their representatives, the priests and elders, were inside, closer to the most sacred space between the T-pillars at the centre of those concentric circles. It is striking also how this liturgical arena is, at the same time, a containing vessel, even a massively defended fortress, almost reminiscent already of those we find many centuries later in the gladiatorial arenas of Imperial Rome: witness the powerfully enclosed entrance tunnel, the containing walls, perhaps designed to keep intended sacrificial victims in, as well as to keep the common people out – out, that is, of the sacred space at the centre, between the twin T-pillars.

Another clue, this one seemingly decisive: in the refuse-pits discovered at the site have been found enormous quantities of animal bones; some, clearly, of comestible animals, consumed in great quantities by the early stone age 'pilgrims' in what are thought to have been carnival-type festivities. However, we remember, licensed transgression, in Girardian theory, leads up to the solemn climax of ritual blood sacrifice. Its function is to let loose the anarchic instincts and desires that the social order contains and regulates; so that the ceremony can then re-enact, in a dreamlike sort of way, the logic of founding murder, as a salvational and identity-bonding event. Thus, we are led to ask: are there any signs of the solemn climax we might expect from carnival – any signs of ritual blood sacrifice?

This point is still under evaluation but it is already clear that other refuse-pits show lesser quantities of non-charred bones from non-comestible animals (in this case, symbolically potent, fearsome, predatory ones) and, mingled with these, many butchered human bones. Both animal and human sacrifice, it seems likely, were practised, perhaps in a series of ritual acts representing a crescendo of sacrificial violence. This crescendo, on a Girardian reading, would have re-enacted symbolically the mimetic crisis and its resolution, thereby exorcising all forms of real-life violence.

That possibility alerts us to other, significantly Girardian, motifs. The 'fearsome' animals depicted are, of course, really frightening, in the immediate and concrete sense that they threaten the lives of hunter-gatherers. However, they are also demonised, i.e. held to be guilty of all the woes afflicting the community, including violence born of intra- or inter-community conflict and perhaps even the perceived violence suffered from acts of cosmic nature (which must have seemed overwhelmingly hostile to Neolithic man emerging from the Ice Age). It is in this sense that the goat, which we find also represented on some of the special portal stones, the ones thought to symbolise a communication with 'the other world', is a 'goat-demon', i.e. a demonised victim or scapegoat. A similar logic is clearly at play in the etymology of the English word itself, deriving most probably from Leviticus chapter sixteen (a scapegoat, we remember, lets you off the hook – it is an 'escape' goat).

If we look at the 'humanised' T-pillars which demarcate the sacred ritual space at the centre, we can see that they bear a sculpted representation of the victim and/or god; perhaps, in their very mirror-like *dédoublement*, they represent the first changed into the second. The pillars are, symbolically, half-human, half-divine and they show the obscure dream logic at work in the sacrificial process itself. A dynamic of transformation is represented which reveals the – quite unconscious – 'pharmacology' Girard has described: a polarity of life forces is here being reversed symbolically, from negative to positive, i.e. from death to life, from disorder to order, from violence to peace. We may notice in passing the T-shape of the pillars; it anticipates the earliest shape taken, in those countries where this judicial sanction came later to be practised, by the cross of crucifixion.

There is a final feature, inscribed in the site as a whole, which is the most curious of all. The standing-stone rings, whatever their function, must have seemed to the Neolithic 'pilgrims' to lose their virtue or their potency because fresh, near-identical structures (albeit, progressively less elaborate) were, over a period of nearly 1,400 years, built nearby or else simply on top of previous constructions (first filled in for the purpose), seemingly in the hope of making good some mysterious-yet-central deficiency:

> Every few decades, people buried the pillars and put up new stones – a second, smaller ring inside the first. Sometimes, later, they installed a third. Then the whole assemblage would be filled

in with debris, and an entirely new circle created nearby. The site may have been built, filled in, and built again for centuries. (Mann, 2011: 48)

In short, the monumental labour that early Neolithic man poured into this temple complex was 'never-ending', since each temple had to be constantly 're-tuned', improved and even replaced (on average every seventy years). Yet, 'bewilderingly', as Charles Mann says, the people at Göbekli Tepe got steadily 'worse at temple building'. The earliest rings are the biggest and most sophisticated, technically and artistically. As time went by, the pillars became smaller, simpler, and were mounted with less and less care. Finally, the effort seems to have petered out altogether: 'by 8,200 BCE, Göbekli Tepe was all fall and no rise' (Mann 2011: 48).

This extraordinary singularity requires explanation and Girard's theory of violent origins supplies it, elegantly and exactly – it is a perfect fit. Perhaps we can see why? The control of violence by emissary victimisation, hence the power of human sacrifice to deliver survival, let alone salvation, is a product of human self-mystification; and it doesn't work. So those Neolithic pilgrims had to begin again, trying harder; they had to fill in the hole, displace the temple, reconstruct it over and over again, in an eternal recurrence of effort and expiation; until hope ran out, the spark died and the people scattered or perished.[8]

---

8. An earlier version of this section (Antonello and Gifford, 2015b:262-288) is discussed parenthetically in Hodder 2019, chapter 5. The review committee concludes that Göbekli Tepe might be assigned 'an important purpose, that of symbolic (?) [sic] sacrifice'; and that the monuments erected there might thus be 'potential key players in keeping the peace in the early Neolithic'. "Therefore in response to Gifford and Antonello (2015: 284), yes, it certainly appears that Girardian theory has a place at the table of further research initiated by Klaus Schmidt at Göbekli Tepe; and the theory is also finding some degree of confirmation in the 'descriptive and empirical' (Hodder, 2019: 122-23). The committee is, however, markedly concerned not to concede prematurely that actual human – or indeed animal – sacrifice took place at this site. The only cogent evidence for the proposal that real blood was shed, it says, comes from similar sites; whereas the 448 human skeletal fragments so far retrieved at this site could have been imported in the backfill from the surrounding countryside [sic]. It dismisses the evidence of symbolism: e.g. images of carnivores and raptors carrying off severed human heads. It does not address evidence of weaponry, or of architecture; or of the infilling and rebuilding. There is clearly room for further discussion, therefore. This should perhaps include wider anthropological perspectives, and 'known unknowns', such as 'the invisibility of the founding murder'. The fundamental debate is between a cognitivist preference for verified

* * *

That is, perhaps, the ultimate figure of sense we can discern at the bottom of Girard's sinkhole. In glimpsing it, we may have reached a turning point – rather like the charioteers in the rather later Roman arena (some 7,000 years later). That arena too was traced out around twin pillars, by then separated out within that much stretched and flattened oval loop which we may perhaps remember from the film *Ben Hur*. Chariots would race along one side of the course, turn around the mark at the end and race back down the other side of the loop. We are now at just at the far turning-mark, heading back towards the finishing line, labelled 'Reconciliation'.

To get there, we have to complete the outline of founding murder traced out in the present chapter and this we may most easily and profitably do by following Girard in his understanding of the Judaeo-Christian scriptures.

---

facts and a hermeneutic of truth as sense-making operational coherence. The ultimate questions remain: why the monumental effort put into these temples by Neolithic man? Whence his fascination, his acknowledged sacrificial obsession?

4
Violence, the Archaic Sacred and Judaeo-Christian Revelation

We move on in this chapter from René Girard's scenario of founding murder to his writings on religion. Many will be surprised to hear the news that any such thing exists in the work of this fundamental anthropologist and culture theorist; and we must, in clarification, start by saying a word about what is, indeed, a relatively little-known face of Girard. How does it come to be, how has it been received – or, rather more often, not received – and why?

How is it that Girard – even if we take as given that he is interested in the sacred, even if he considers that humanity is 'born out of the religious dimension of things' – came to be also an avid decipherer and commentator of the Judaeo-Christian scriptures? It should be noted that the latter part of his work, from *Things Hidden* onwards, is almost entirely devoted to re-introducing the Old and New Testaments into the intellectual mainstream (from which the near entirety of modern critical theory in the last third of the twentieth century had appeared to banish them forever). Furthermore, this dimension of his work is evidently so important to him personally that he says in his last book *Battling to the End*: 'all of my books have been more or less explicit apologies for Christianity. I would like this one to be even more explicit' (*BE* 2010: xv).[1]

---

1. This declaration implies and supposes a personal faith-commitment which R.G. has sometimes consented to discuss. See Girard *QCC* 1994: 191-226 and Girard *EC* 2007: 44-45, in which R.G. writes notably: 'It is not because I am a Christian that I think as I do; it is because of my research that I became a Christian. I also question the distinction between an intellectual and an emotional conversion. As for St Paul, the word "spirit" includes for me both the emotional and the

This declaration would most certainly have surprised the French secularist critic who, hailing in *Le Monde* (27 October 1972) the appearance of Girard's first work of cultural anthropology, the ground-breaking *Violence and the Sacred*, suggested this was the most significant work of atheism in the twentieth century.

Why did he think so? It seemed to him evident that Girard was offering to accomplish what Freud, Marx and Nietzsche had between them failed to do: namely, to account adequately, without God, for the genesis on earth of the phenomenon of religion. In other words, this critic was supposing Girard to be engaged in working out a psycho-poetics of socially-generated, wholly man-made religion, the principal import of which would, of course, be to reduce all manifestations of the sacred to one long, if increasingly elaborate, man-made God-delusion, identical at bottom to the earliest self-mystifying form it takes in the scenario of founding murder, with its dreamlike sacralisation of the scapegoat victim. One imagines Richard Dawkins applauding this project vigorously, and Christopher Hitchens nodding enthusiastically – only, then, to turn suddenly thoughtful.

The viewpoint advanced does indeed labour under a considerable difficulty; and the joke was on this French critic. More exactly, it was on his premature, mimetically suggestive reception of 'the death of God'. Its author was, moreover, trapped within a presupposition entirely characteristic of French secularism: he thought that all religions were contained in, and sufficiently explained by, the ill-defined category of 'the sacred', and that deciphering this talisman must be the key to the atheistic reduction of the entire set of them.

Girard, on the contrary, thinks of the sacred (synonyms: 'the archaic sacred', 'natural religion') as a first-form, a substratum or a residual lining of the more organised polytheisms which came later (synonyms: 'sacrificial religions', 'pagan religions'); and he takes these in turn as precursor forms of the emergent Abrahamic faiths (French secularists would call these 'monotheisms') which came along after that.

Moreover, what essentially interests Girard is not a taxonomy as such of all religions (i.e. a classification of types), it is – in sheer fascination – the wondrous particularity that differentiates from what he calls the archaic sacred – the transformed themes and dynamics which he finds illustrated specifically in the Hebrew scriptures

---

intellectual side of a human being; and, rather than "intellectual", the expression "the life of the mind" should be used in this instance. Conversion is a form of intelligence, of understanding.'

(Christianity's Old Testament) and, above all, in the Gospels. (Girard subscribes absolutely to the dictum that Christianity is 'the religion of the Gospel'.)

This conceptual framing of his thought is worth a moment's further attention. Christianity is not – save at first sight, according to a misleading generic taxonomy and/or by convention – '*a* religion' (i.e. one among others). Nor is it '*the* religion' (i.e. the only one – since 'religion' comes in thousands of varieties). Nor is it, either, '*no kind of* religion' (a 'faith' but not a religion, for instance). It is, or it is nothing, the religion and faith, conjoined and interdependent, of the Gospel.

Girard has also, be it noted, written one short but vital book extending his purview to a consideration of sacrifice in the Hindu Vedanta scriptures (2015) but he makes no claims to be a specialist of comparative religion, in the sense which prevails in academe. What he does claim, in the filmed interview ('From Animal to Human'), the transcript of which is reproduced in the Appendix to this book, is that Christianity stands apart from the mythologies and religions of the archaic sacred. They stem, he says, from the scapegoat mechanism misinterpreted; Christianity is the same mechanism correctly interpreted. It represents, therefore, a demystification; it is a novelty in the history of emergent – and, foundationally, universally religious (i.e. archaic-sacral) – humanity.

Girard is, indeed, led by his fascination for the emergence of novelty: a novelty he sees at work transforming the mythologies, rites and laws of archaic-sacral or pagan religions. He sees, in this one very particular developmental line or *phylum* of religious experience, thought and practice, a prodigious breaking up, and a re-writing, of the very violent logic of archaic sacrality – in fact, of that primordial 'programming' of group intelligence operating in emergent, culturally developing, humankind. His fascination is a perpetual: 'Aha! – so that's how the Light gets in . . . '

Always, this emergence of novelty is read by Girard as a recasting of the common 'syntax' or 'grammar' (so to speak) of the archaic sacred. That's how 'revelation' in a Jewish or Christian sense can be recognised, identified and reliably understood to be light and grace from above; that's how the Darwinian logic of survival, with the archaic sacralities it generates, is transformed, and becomes elevated into a genuine work of salvation.

In the interview of 2009 referred to above, Girard vigorously agrees that most of us are prone to assume that 'religion' must be either 'natural' (i.e. man-made) or else 'supernatural' (i.e. God-given). What we urgently need to get our heads around, all of us, is the probability that both things may be – are most fundamentally likely to be – true! Isn't that what we should expect to find in a free, evolutionary and emergent creation which, like humanity itself, is coming to be?

For the larger part of the two and a half millennia or so since the biblical text entitled 'Genesis' was written, it has been assumed that that text was limited to describing how our earthly habitat once and for all sprang into being and how the appearance in it of humanity too came about once and for all, historically, within the same uniform history of world process. The awakening in the nineteenth century of evolutionary and wider cosmological perspectives has, over the past century or so, liberated the theological imagination – at least, in the case of non-fundamentalist believers – from the mental cramp of historical literalism; revealing them, on the one hand, the part of anthropomorphism and myth which will be latent in all unexamined assumptions (including theological ones) but also, and more significantly, how the big picture of Genesis is true in a far wider and deeper sense than had been previously thought – true 'always in principle'.

In just this way, Girard does all people of faith the immense service of allowing them to re-imagine for our time the relationship between God and His creation. Providing we avoid the surprisingly common confusion which consists of thinking anthropology is, or ought to be, do and say the same thing as theology, greater truth will be seen to emerge from myth, penetrated by the light that arises from outside the myth's horizons, only to transcend and transform those confines and modifying in the process the mythologising and sacralising human subject. In the Girardian vision of things, we are free to learn and we learn by opening up to the light from above, and by an ever more faithfully enacted mimesis of theological imagination ('Thy Kingdom come . . . on earth as it is in Heaven').

Is that not how revelation itself actually works? If we're genuinely interested, moreover, in reconciliation, in acting together with people of other faiths and none, to transform human relationships long mortgaged to acquisitive, conflictual and antagonistic mimesis and to the conflict of local or tribal altruisms – but capable of eventually opening the way to the hope of a common, even a universal, salvation – then, I would venture to suggest, that is exactly the type of roadmap we most urgently need.

* * *

Now, Girard is a superb reader and explicator of texts but he is not a systematising philosopher. There may well be a grand narrative to be found in his work but he's not himself the system-building articulator and theorist of it. Had he been to that particular manor born, he would have penned a superior version of the prologue I have just offered and he would immediately, then, have discussed how his fundamental anthropology and Judaeo-Christian theology come together to read the story of human origins, the story given in the account of Creation in Genesis chapter one and the story of the Temptation and Fall in chapters two and three.[2]

What is the difference – this 'missing' prologue would have asked – between our two perspectives on the sacred? Between your theology and my anthropology? Do we see this difference between accounts as a conflictual difference or is it a complementary one, an illuminating and dialogic difference?

What an encounter that missing chapter on Genesis would have been! The Bible's Edenic prologue is built around the very formula of that Girardian mimetic triangle. It is built, that is, around the structural figure which describes the dynamic interrelation between two subjects whose hands reach out in rivalry for the same Object, one of them acting as mediator to the other whose desire he interiorises and copies (mimesis). It is the same schema that is represented here, save that, for the first time in the history of human thinking, the triangle is powerfully relativised from above. There is a prior Subject of Desire and an order of creation – there is the Creator God. Within the order of Creation, it is human mimetic rivalry with God that is being staged; and which is being presented now as the fact and the fault of mimetically suggestible, blame-shifting, mis-sacralising humankind.

How suggestive it is that Adam, challenged by the Lord God, offloads the blame for their common rivalry of disobedience onto Eve, who in turn blames the serpent. Where will the buck stop? We have here three successive suggestions for what French calls a '*bouc émissaire*' (our own word 'buck' is connected, etymologically, to that French expression for 'scapegoat') and what those successive suggestions of deflected blame point back to is the human propensity for moral obliquity and evasiveness. They

---

2. It must be said in Girard's defence that he never fully shared the culturally conditioned perception of Protestant Britain and America that Darwin represented a fundamental, crisis-bearing challenge to Christianity: see his replies on this subject in the interview 'From Animal to Human' reproduced in the Appendix.

designate the all-too-immediate and self-mystifying disguise of injured innocence which is part of our evolutionary default setting: 'What, me, Guv?!? Not me, Guv, him!!' (and, especially, of course, her!!!).

On the subject of human mis-sacralisations of the objects of desire, the author of *Deceit Desire and the Novel* is already fixed. Discussing the syndrome of exclusion and fascinated adoration, linking Proust's narrator to the 'little band' in which figures the beloved Albertine, Girard quotes Louis Ferrero: 'Passion is the change of address of a force which Christianity has awoken and oriented towards God' (*DDN* 1965: 75). He adds: 'the negation of God does not suppress that transcendence, but it causes it to deviate from the beyond to the this-earthly'; stating further that 'as heaven becomes uninhabited, the sacred flows back over the earth . . . deviated transcendence is the caricature of vertical transcendence' (*DDN* 1965: 78) .

That perspective of deviated transcendence is precisely the novel framework brought by Genesis (and the whole of the Hebrew scriptures) to the cults born around our neighbour the victim; son or daughter of the hidden founding murder. If human desire has a true Object, the deviant variety, born of distance, exclusion and prohibition, is a mimetic fantasm and a form of rivalrous mimetic idolatry.

What, then, of the mediator, that older and deeper Other voice itself? Intimate to ourselves, but here externalised mythically, and very plausibly represented as denizen of the archaic shadow-zone or shudder-zone within us – namely, the serpent? Do we not want to say that this voice is, in fact, misrecognised as 'other'; that he is, in fact, our own, older (i.e. evolutionary and animal) otherness?[3] That voice speaks in rivalry, because it speaks – not after the order of Creation, but within the frame which human desire projects for itself, in its own image and likeness; it speaks in the self-sacralising and transgressive logic of the archaic sacred.

---

3. Naturalist Sir David Attenborough has recently shown to British TV audiences a memorable instance of 'serpent cunning' which elucidates profoundly – and in mimetic terms – the complementarity of evolutionary and theological perspectives to which Girard is pointing. The viper native to the very hot rocky deserts of Iran has developed a breathtaking hunting strategy: not only does it camouflage itself so as to imitate perfectly the colours and asperities of its natural setting, but it has developed a tail with trailing 'strings' and an abdomen-type tip, which it has learned to display and agitate so as to imitate the jerky movements of the local desert spiders. Migrating birds are fascinated and come down to catch the 'spiders', only to get swallowed by the snake they have failed to see. (BBC I-Player, 'Seven Worlds, One Planet', series1:2, 'Asia' [22.34-27.30]; accessed December 2019). The Sacred is continuous with the violent logic of evolutionary *survival* (whereas *salvation* is a new beginning 'from above').

Eve has interiorised – 'copied' – the desire of the serpent and, in doing so, she enters into mimetic rivalry with God. Or, at least, with the distorted and archaic representation the serpent has of God – namely, as power-holder and sacraliser of the human moral and social order; hence, the repressive killjoy of human inventiveness, aspiration and autonomy.

That survival-born instinct of competitive advantage, that serpent-inheritance, what does it become at the threshold of hominisation, at the point where it accedes decisively to a certain self-awareness? Girard's collaborator and fellow author of *Things Hidden*, Michel Oughourlian suggests an answer: 'The serpent, in whom Christian tradition has recognised the Evil One, the Devil, the Prince of this world, is the mimetic principle inasmuch as it perverts human relations and creates rivalry' (Oughourlian 2007: 37).

Once we grasp these implications of mimetic theory, the sense of the Temptation is subtly enriched and deepened. 'Evil' – I quote here the very 'received' Anglican orthodoxy of Tom Wright – 'consists in . . . the rebellious idolatry by which humans worship and honour elements of the created world rather than the God who made them' (Wright 2007: 106). That's a characteristically robust assertion: valuable in what it asserts; less so, perhaps, in what it leaves out of account (can we localise evil so exactly?) and is it, perhaps, a touch conventional? Is this not to invoke the stern autocrat and powerbroker: the feudal Governor of Creation, whom the writers of Genesis may indeed have believed in, but who, after Darwin, is much more difficult for us to affirm without qualification; the sort of 'God' the serpent, for his part, would very much like us to believe in – the better to incite us to launch our bid for that transgressively godlike thrill or 'high'?

More exactly stated, what the text itself invites us to conclude is that mimetic rivalry, rather than rebellion is the most intimately founding spring and inspiration of evil. It is our falling for the delusory promise, with its part of shadow and its poisoned fruit: 'Ye shall be as gods, knowing good and evil.'

The expression 'as gods' which figures in the mirific promise of the serpent points us very much to the moral ambiguity of human pre-eminence in nature. It tells us, as Girard also does, that the potential of the mimetic creature for godlikeness is also a potential for diabolical evil. We can all agree with that, perhaps. However, what a Girardian reading sniffs out here, more acutely than most, is that this ambiguity must have been sounded out and known via some concrete experience of 'ersatz' transcendence, something both coveted and idolised in preference to the high and holy Creator God of Israel. Surely, the plural 'gods', and the cautionary adverb of quasi-similitude 'as gods', give us a sufficient hint to what it was? They connote the environing context of Canaanite polytheism: that rival sacrality of orgies and child sacrifice, of blood lust and of the erotic thrill of manipulating the power of life and death.

If we take account of this subtly indicated but perceptible critique of a parallel and rival sacrality, what then? Then we understand rather better where the Bible starts from, where it is coming from, and how Genesis is put together. It speaks to proclaim as the starting point of the human adventure, the high and holy Creator's bringing-into-being of a world of order and purpose: a garden of plenty and delight, a created Other of beauty and splendour. It speaks also, however, to warn humankind of our propensity to spoil and destroy that goodness from within our freedom and it does the warning a touch obsessively (anxiously, hence excessively) by way of a reactive insistence stiffened by a pre-encountered resistance.

Even to the point of shifting all the blame for the world's evil, uncompromisingly, as a job lot, onto human shoulders and, in the process, projecting heavenwards a residually wrathful and punitive image of God. That image is still close to the 'monstrous double' generated by the implicit mimetic rivalry we have glimpsed behind the text. If we were to make hyper-explicit the problem this creates, we might even say the blame is shifted as a Job lot; since it is in the book of Job that the unexamined residue of the problem left by the writers of Genesis is picked up and thematised.

'Accursedness' (in labour and in childbirth), like exile from Eden itself, are still presented in this text as divine condemnations or punishments; even if these things are also shown, clearly enough, to be self-inflicted human wounds; even as they signify *de facto* a prohibition placed on the greatest Object of sacralising and rivalrous human desire; even as they proclaim an exile that must surely, in all sound logic of Genesis, be first of all a function of the interval of unlikeness between heaven and earth, God's sphere and ours. (We think again here of our Lord's prayer: 'Thy Kingdom come . . . on earth, as it is in Heaven'.)

Overall, however, we can see, that Genesis steps, momentously, outside the world of the archaic sacred. It recognises and refers to it; it represents and critiques it – in the name of the Lord God who made would-be sapiens and under whose judgement wanna-be sapiens henceforth stands. If we accept fully that evolutionary anthropology and theology have distinct starting points and perspectives of interpretation, the accounts they offer are by no means contradictory. They are, on the contrary, mutually illuminating and wondrously complementary.

Once we get that, we can see why certain Christian theologians who take Girard to task for his 'darkened' or 'bleak' theological vision, or who 'struggle with his negativity', hinting darkly at gnostic filiations, are missing the point grievously. Developing this realisation, we may even come to see how we might be led, on the path pioneered by his reading, to restate the Augustinian version of original sin. ('Fall' is going to rhyme henceforth with 'call' and not just with 'all' – but that is another day's labour.)[4]

It is becoming, at all events, distinctly *passé* to stress the supposedly problematic or contentious nature of Girard's biblical commentaries. They are becoming very widely accepted and used, for instance, within the Catholic faculty of theology at Innsbruck and, as we saw, by theologians contributing to *La Croix* in France. They are very widely quoted, too, in exegeses pursued by Protestant theologians in Britain and the United States. If we care to look up the entry 'sacrifice', for example, in Eerdmans *Dictionary of the Bible*, we shall find that this entire article is constructed specifically and nominally around a Girardian understanding.

Reception of Girard by Christian theologians will depend, really, on how aware they are of the need for a post-Darwinian perspective and how far they agree to focus on an anthropology of emergent religious truth (i.e. of divine self-communication in historical time). It will depend also on the theologian's greater or lesser ability to think flexibly (in both interdisciplinary and transformational senses); and, of course, it will depend on his or her having read and actually knowing Girard's theory adequately. These are quite demanding conditions. However, they are increasingly being satisfied and, already, it will be widely agreed that Girard offers a rare vision of survival 'opened up' to salvation.

I must now try to offer some glimpses of this reading at work and of its potential for reconciliation: first, in the Hebrew scriptures (the Christian Old Testament); then in the gospels (around which is modelled the Christian New Testament).

---

4. This labour of exploration has been undertaken by Jack Mahoney (2011) and by James Alison (1998): see Cited Texts and Further Reading, p. 139. The question of Girard's own view is touched on in Chapter 4, p. 58 and explored in the Appendix, p. 136.

***

Predictably, the beginnings of the Jewish Bible (and the Christian Old Testament) confront us with a horizon of primitive religious-cultural practice entirely recognisable from other mythologies. Echoes of disorder run through all the major stories of Genesis and Exodus: Temptation and Fall; the tower of Babel; Sodom and Gomorrah; the ten plagues of Egypt. Noah's flood, which has distinct parallels in Babylonian and even in Greek myth,[5] is perhaps, in part, a metaphor for mimetic crisis (plague and flood often have this undeclared exchange-value in world mythologies). The founding murder re-echoes in these texts: fatefully committed by one warring brother against another (Cain and Abel); the victimisation of Joseph by his brothers; the humano-divine struggle between Jacob and the angel. We observe a nation's descent into internal and external conflict, the removal of differences and hierarchies which constitute the community in its wholeness; there is the all against one of collective violence; there is the development of prohibitions and rituals. As echo-located by all these multiple traces, the generative matrix of the archaic sacred is entirely recognisable as a conditioning context of emergence.

Far from being embarrassed by the residual presence in the Judaeo-Christian scriptures of this matrix of the archaic sacred, and of mythological elements shared with world religions, Girard goes out of his way to underline these things: such shared beginnings serve, precisely, to measure an original and far more remarkable pattern of textual and historical emergence, which, as he demonstrates with impressive rigour of exegesis, asserts itself increasingly as the scriptural story unfolds.

Elementarily, what we observe is that the editors of the first books of the Bible reshape their material, setting up a new perspective, a new pattern. Temptation and Fall? They set out, as we have observed, the very formula of the mimetic triangle. Could humanity, after all, be its own victimiser – the real violator, the real generating agent of sacred violence?

Cain, though he founds a culture (the Canaanite culture), is not presented as justified in killing his brother – unlike Romulus, founder of Rome. Where is his murdered brother, whose blood 'cries out from the ground' to God? It cries, not for vengeance, but for room to declare the truth of the founding murder, acknowledging explicitly what archaic-sacral ritual asserts implicitly, that a limit must be set to the

---

5. These echoes are to be found in the Babylonian Epic of Gilgamesh and in the Greek myth of Deucalion's ark.

corrupting contagion of violence – such is the 'mark of Cain'. Here is a prohibition on violent reprisal or retaliation pointing towards the development of the Law itself, with its more radical commandment 'Thou shalt not kill'.[6]

Critical clarity, moral truthfulness, subversive re-writing also fashion the Bible's equivalent of the Oedipus story. If he had been presented in the mythological framework of the archaic sacred, Joseph would have been depicted as a hubristic and patricidal power-plotter, justly punished by his righteous brothers. (His dreams in fact suggest how the alternative version would have started and the possibility of a fully 'sacrificial' account is further hinted at in the Biblical story by Joseph's bloodied coat, presented to the father to explain his 'disappearance'.)

To say here, with Max Weber, that Jewish writings 'always side with victims', Jews having so often found themselves battered and bruised by history, is a woefully prejudicial half-truth, inadequately responding to this powerful novelty. What careful cross-cultural comparison reveals is that the tangled threads of the archaic sacred are here being partially unravelled, that responsibility for violence is being tentatively laid at the right address – and that archaic sacrifices cannot any more serve as a universal symbolic expedient for patching up potentially violent religious, political and socio-economic crises (*TH* 1987: 147).

From the beginning, in short, Biblical texts are engaged in demystifying the archaic sacred: deciphering its dubious credit transfer operations, discrediting its declared villains, vindicating its vilified victims and even, little by little, contradicting its self-generated theology of sacred violence.

That is the master pattern of the Girardian reading; and this process gathers pace throughout the Old Testament. It is enough to think of Islamic State today to see at once why deconstructing a self-generated theology of sacred violence might be a rather vital sort of thing to be doing. At all events, today's occasions of 'shock-horror' are very much already happening in some texts of the Hebrew scriptures. Which perhaps raises this strategic and pertinent question: does it take the prism of the Gospels, applied retrospectively, to recognise this type of

---

6. Girard suggests that ritual is the place where tradition and innovation meet. He instances the sacrifice of Isaac, which 'announces the renunciation of human sacrifice and the passage towards animal sacrifice'. 'The extraordinary thing about the Biblical text is that it begins by presenting an Abraham who is still following the system of human sacrifice. It shows the obedience first; it shows that, from that obedience, truthful change is possible' (*QCC* 1994: 84).

antecedence and to discern the subterranean action of Grace in the Old Testament's movement beyond such patterns of attitude and behaviour? Or is some such discernment available to the best insight of all three traditions of inheritance from Abraham? (This latter hypothesis is explored in Kirwan and Achtar, 2019.)

What we observe in the texts themselves is that ritual human sacrifice is replaced, structurally speaking, by the Covenant, in anticipation, and/or in consequence of which, that religious institution modulates into animal sacrifice. When Abraham resolves to sacrifice Isaac, the original 'archaic' practice is, in collective memory, still close at hand. What is new is that the patriarch trusts in a God who provides for a substitutionary animal offering. The archaic ritual is then progressively inflected. Divine mercy can be influenced by penitential sin-offerings; the episode of Leviticus 16, where the scapegoat makes his first nominal appearance in the Jewish scriptures has to do with this modulation of sacrificial practice. When, on the annual Day of Atonement (Yom Kippur) the scapegoat Azazel is symbolically charged with bearing away the sins of the whole people, he illustrates the logic of archaic sacrifice exactly – albeit with this perfecting amendment, that the other goat then offered to Yahweh becomes a pure offering, freed from the taint borne off by the scapegoat.

Primitive sacrificial practice has again been revised, re-interpreted (as it is again, more fundamentally, in the inward sacrifice of praise). It can then be religiously displaced and in part replaced ('I desire mercy, not sacrifice', as Hosea 6:6 has it). Yet, as Girard often reminds us, Leviticus 16 does not yet understand scapegoating as the European sixteenth and seventeenth centuries came to understand it; it does not yet see in emissary victimisation a symbolic and self-serving manipulation. It is still embedded in – and, in some measure, at some level, still committed to – the practice of blame-transfer (i.e. it is, residually, still a transactional and quasi-magical solution of the problem of human guilt).

Prohibition becomes Law, which, remarkably, begins to transcend the fearful barrier protecting Israel's self-differentiation. In place of the scrupulous minutiae of ritual purity detailed in Leviticus, it produces the magisterial ethico-spiritual simplicity of the 'Decalogue'. This sovereign codification of the 'words of God' identifies exactly and without remainder all proximate objects of mimetic rivalry between men, supplying in addition a corrective to the self-deceiving untruth that founds the world of the sacred ('Thou shalt not bear false witness'); and, naming (at least) the all-sufficient antidote-in-principal to all conflictual mimesis, divine 'words' numbers one and two (i.e. the first and second commandments) indeed, make love of neighbour a corollary to the love of God.

Via the troubled rule of the sacral kings of Israel, the unfolding pattern of biblical originality produces at length the post-exilic prophets, who focus the potential and promise of Israel's special vocation among the nations in the figure of the suffering servant. Against the background of intense political threat and devastation, failing theocratic institutions and renewed internal crisis, this recapitulative figure develops in symbiosis and in tension with the first (this-worldly) Messaianic figuration, derived from the archaic sacred: that of the triumphant military ruler, who will reverse the subjection, humiliation and distress of Israel; so that the last shall become first, and the victim people will begin again on the right side of history. 'So the three great pillars of primitive religion – myth, sacrifice and prohibitions – are subverted by the thought of the Prophets' (*TH* 1987: 155).

Meanwhile, the book of Job, supremely, gives voice to the victim. It stages in dialogue with the victim himself the entire ambivalence of the archaic sacred. Ultimately, as Girard shows us, it wrests the deity out of the process of persecution to envision him instead as the God of the oppressed and the downtrodden. The victim here is an incomplete *figura Christi* but, for the first time, he can say: 'I know that my redeemer liveth' (Job 19:25). God, as shown here, paradigmatically, and for the first time, is seen to prefer a man who speaks the truth to one who blames the sufferer for his sufferings in order to safeguard the moral reputation of God. The truth of Job is that the high and holy God, unlike the tribal deity often mistaken for Him, is not vengeful.

Girard applies integrally to this text the deconstructivist thrust of his own theory of the archaic sacred. The X-ray shape he discerns beneath the fabulating and still mythic data of the story is that Job is the 'victim of his people'. In other words, the God with whom Job wrestles is not just that of a peculiar Hebrew tradition of retributive justice (given voice by the so-called 'friends of Job'), he is, in part still, the sacralised projection of the 'God' of the archaic sacred (or 'primitive religion') as such, i.e. a monstrous double, required, engendered and consecrated by man's ancient, devious and universal game of exorcising violently his own violent shadow; which fearsome deity, born of the social psyche, constitutes, in evolutionary terms, the inherited default setting of man 'the sacralising animal'.

The Book of Job stages, in fact, the entire ambivalence of the archaic sacred and its 'containment' of violence, and it epitomises the gradual – and sometimes fitful – Hebraic 'verticalisation' of *homo religiosus*.

Isaiah's suffering servant, for his part, is the pure embodiment of the victim-figure as saviour: rejected scapegoat of all, discharging the community of all its sins and all its violence, strikingly recapitulative in his complete innocence, his otherness in relation to all the ills offloaded onto him. He thematises, for the first time, explicitly and comprehensively, the covert operation of blame-transfer associated with founding murder. The scapegoat theme, in short, is here considered strategically in relation to the entire enterprise of salvation.

In all these texts, the ferment of subversive novelty, challenging, reworking and replacing elements of the archaic sacred, is in principle clear. Yet, not even in the conception of the suffering servant (sometimes still described, in an apparent lapse into archaism, as the expiatory victim *of God*[7]) can the process be said to have been carried through to its logical term. The sacrificial temple survives and, with it, the legal prohibitions, the mythical stories and the theocratic state. Above all, a monstrous double survives: the God of the archaic sacrificial system: the wrathful, retributive and often bloodthirsty Jehovah of Hebrew tribal imagining – and, naturally enough, if we have followed and properly understood Girard – of ours! (How important it will be, in matters of reconciliation, to start from that common ground). Girard summarises the case: 'Yet all the same, in the Old Testament we never arrive at a conception of the deity that is entirely foreign to violence. . . . Yahweh is still the God to whom vengeance belongs. The notion of divine retribution is still alive' (*TH* 1987: 157-58).

Now here, Girard has given us a demonstration of extraordinary pertinence. The Girardian reading prepares us to understand something crucial: namely, that the immense place accorded to violence represented in the Judaeo-Christian scriptures, in excess even of that accorded it in Greek tragedy, is part of the unfolding pattern of originality and is

---

7. A whole number of passages lay upon men the principal responsibility of his saving death. One of these even appears to attribute to men the exclusive responsibility for that death: 'Yet we esteemed him stricken, smitten by God, and afflicted' (Isaiah 53:4). In other words, this was not so. It was not God who smote him; God's responsibility is implicitly denied'. And yet: 'Even in the most advanced texts, such as the Fourth Song of the Servant. there is still some ambiguity about the role of Yahweh . . . God himself is the presented as the principal instigator of the persecution: 'Yet it was the will of the Lord to bruise him' (Isaiah 53:10).

a mark, not so much of a special and suspect affiliation to violence, but of an exceptionally acute anthropological awareness and a singular honesty about sacred violence *per se*. The Bible does not simply ask us to pity victims, not even to pity Israel as principal victim among the nations. Its originality lies rather in the way it addresses and grapples with the deep-laid and obscure foundational link between, on the one hand, human violence and its making of victims and, on the other, the human (culturally generated) order of religion and society.

* * *

We come now to Girard's reading of the gospels. It will be convenient to examine first Jesus' teaching on violence and the attestation of the ministry of teaching and healing. Then I'd like to say something about what links together, for Girard, in one single weave, the teaching and healing ministry, on the one hand, and, on the other, the climactic events of Cross and Resurrection (events which will occupy us more searchingly in our next chapter).

Girard's reading of the gospels starts from the notion that Jesus Messiah enters a conflicted, violent and blood-soaked world. He addresses that world with a counter-proposal; which his proclamation of the Kingdom of Heaven, first, and then, more radically, his Passion will enact. What is specific to Girard's commentary is that his scenario of founding murder helps him read, as it were, 'over the shoulder' of Jesus, a response-in-faith which recognises the truth about founding murder and, ultimately, re-enters that same original scenario of archaic-sacral religion, in order to lift its fatality from humankind.

Jesus, Girard sees acutely, is addressing a world in which conflict and violence are painfully endemic. Roman domination consistently and contemptuously inflicts at sword-point all sorts of casual humiliations on Jews. Villagers could indeed be required carry a legionary's pack, weighing, with full armour, weaponry, cooking and digging utensils, around 30 kilos. (By way of comparison, Ryanair allow us 22 kilos of hold baggage and most of us, deprived of our luggage trolleys, could not carry that load 50 yards. So much for going 'the extra mile'!) Such exactions – like taxation and (of course) crucifixion – were part of the so-called *Pax Romana*. Jesus would have seen how Jewish rebelliousness, already evidenced in the Maccabean wars of recent memory, responded to that violence done to body and spirit (violence comes in different forms and at different levels). However, there is also criminal violence:

we think of the man robbed and beaten by brigands, who is tended by the good Samaritan. There was also vicious sectarian infighting between religious factions (Pharisees, Saducees, Essenes, Herodians, Galilleans, Baptists) and, of course, renewed and sporadic nationalist insurgencies. Luke tells us (13:1) of the fate of one pilgrimage of Galileans at Passover time, probably just a couple of years or so before the events of Holy Week; the group was identified as harbouring terrorists (as we would say today) and bloodily repressed within the Temple precincts.

When people are insecure – and during a military occupation, even if it is exercised in part by proxy, that applies to both occupied and occupiers – then they become jumpy and they react badly. Herod, placeholder of the Roman occupiers and paranoid oriental despot, reacted badly, as we remember. The coming among us of the Prince of Peace induced in him a paroxysm of murderous violence, massacring the Innocents in Bethlehem. In telling this story, Matthew means us to hear – and Girard, for his part, remembers profoundly – Rachel weeping once more for her children (Matthew 2:18). Violence: as in the time of the Assyrian destruction of the Northern Kingdom; as in the savage capture of Jerusalem by King Nebuchadnezzar of Babylon; as will again be the case in the great Jewish rebellion of 66-70 CE, which ended with the truly apocalyptic siege and sack of Jerusalem and its hinterland by the legions of Vespasian and Titus. Jewish historian Josephus tells us of large-scale massacres, unspeakable atrocities and a stone by stone levelling of the second Temple.

That ultimate cataclysm in which unlimited violence is visited on Israel is distinctly foreseen by Jesus in the gospels. He sees it in the perspective of Israel's failure to respond to the other way of the Kingdom of Heaven; rejecting the Messiah, Jerusalem will have not known 'the things that belong to its peace' (Luke 19:42).

Certainly, the *Pax Romana* ruled. This so-called peace kept the lid on private and inter-ethnic forms of violence; it maintained public order by force. However, in the process of doing so, or more exactly (in structural terms) in order to do it, Roman order recycled and, indeed, institutionalised violence. We need only think of what the judicial instrument of crucifixion does to its victims and of why it is required to do that. The Empire sacralised Roman might and it actually came to divinise its supreme power holders, the emperors. The punishment of those who threatened or defied that form of the sacred on which the political, legal and moral order rested, had to be a conspicuous exercise of sacral violence, both exemplary and terrible.

That judicial instrument of crucifixion is a classic case of what Girard means by the legacy of founding murder. 'Bloody spectacle' remained the ultimate foundation of the sacred majesty of law and order, even in England, up to and well beyond Shakespeare's time. What we observe here also is that earlier ages had their own forms of our own 'absolute' or 'nuclear' deterrent; a calculated dose of precisely targeted, ritualised violence, or the threat of it, holding at bay ('containing') a wider more cataclysmic violence, in which we can discern still the underlying basic pattern of founding murder.

Jesus will end up at that same point – as victim – and he will do so by the very fact of addressing consequentially, to the end, the crux of founding murder itself. However, he begins by proclaiming the Kingdom of Heaven and teaching about the sources of violence in the human heart. The Beatitudes point to something striking. Human violence, observably, rebounds between adversaries, in the form of a tit-for-tat reciprocity. I do to you, preferably with interest, what you do to me (or, in the case of judicial retribution, at one remove, 'for what you did to him/her/them,etc.'). We usually recognise this dynamic of mimetic reciprocity by the formula inherited from the Old Testament: 'an eye for an eye, a tooth for a tooth'. That is the so-called *lex talionis*: the principle of just and permitted retribution.

The point about those proclamations of 'blessedness' – i.e. unsuspected godlikeness, receptivity to grace – is that they subvert our natural human reaction of violent riposte to the violence practised against us; most particularly, they subvert the tendency to sacralise our own second-phase or defensive violence and call it 'justified' and 'just'. They advocate – not passivity, that is a common misconception which Christian preachers, if they know their onions, will constantly wish to dispel – but non-violent protest against violence and ethical action to overcome it peacefully.

However, we forget (usually) that the real intention of this principle of the Law is to regulate conflict, by restricting at par the human and social damage done. You shall take *only* an eye for an eye, *only* a tooth for a tooth. The whole point is to put a cap on that fearsome dynamic of reciprocal mimetic contagion and escalation. What is crucial is to dampen down that raging tit-for-tat, propagating like wildfire or like plague, and developing exponentially (as we say) towards some terminal paroxysm. That's the thing that is truly death-dealing; it's what puts at risk the very survival of groups, communities, nations – and today, of humankind itself.

So, blessed are the peacemakers, the meek in spirit, those who turn the other cheek, those who mourn for justice undone or fatally injured by the law of the strongest. These things are not directed against anger, as such (especially not as occasioned by legitimate moral outrage or protest), but against sacred rage, bringing retaliation, incremental contagion and apocalypse.

We can see that the Beatitudes are complicit with Girardian perspectives: mimetic desire, founding murder, scapegoating, our common human propensity to shift blame; but also our tendency to exclusionary victimisation, our moral blindness and the partial and unreliable obliquity of the moral insight we do have. That complicity is already surprising enough; but more surprising still, perhaps, is the way in which Girardian analyses, in turn, allow modern minds to enter into the depth and pertinence of the Beatitudes.

Do they help us understand Jesus also in his actual encounters with human violence? Well, here are just a few of the very interesting cases Girard comments on:

The Woman Taken in Adultery (John 8:1-11). The Mosaic code allowed then – and Islamic sharia law permits now – the violent repression, by stoning to death, of sexual errancy, particularly female. What does Jesus do? He writes in the sand, as if his doodling could decipher this mystery of death-dealing sacred rage in God's representatives. More surely still, says Girard, his sand-writing is a nonconfrontational response. It's about not engaging the accusers' glance of sacred fury, not provoking the Beast of self-sacralising rage and sacred violence by direct contradiction, immediate confrontation. (Do reconcilers need to learn from this?) Then comes the decisive test, separating the sacred and the holy: does your own moral purity give you the right to cast stones; or are you simply caught up in the contagion of lynch-mob violence?

The Gerasene Demoniac (Mark 5:1-20; Luke 8:26-39; see S 1986: 165-83). Legion is the traumatised and demented witness of Roman punitive reprisals for Jewish uprisings; he utters the interiorised screaming that resounds within him and has taken him over; he is therefore excluded as dangerous by the community, which fears further cruel reprisals; and, interiorising that reaction, he self-harms in consequence – cutting himself with flints. These deliberately sharpened stones mirror, and interiorise, the 'stoning' that is his exclusionary rejection by the local community – he is, in this sense, the victim of a redoubled scapegoating. The art of healing, says Girard, operates by understanding and compassion; it lifts the curse, cures the spirit and sends the superviolent demons of the human psyche back to their simple animal origins. Jesus is here expelling Hebrew 'demonism', as well as healing the real and actual demons of one aggrieved and grieving human spirit (while the people of Gerasa, in chasing Jesus away, are asserting their need for scapegoats). Legion, in the language of the Beatitudes, is one who 'mourns' violently.

The Lament over Jerusalem (Luke 19:41-44). Jesus is reading, with the lamentations of Jeremiah in mind, the recurrent cycle of violence, which has led Israel to ultimate catastrophe and which looms again cataclysmically, threatening to submerge the worn-out pharmacology of blood-sacrifice practised still in self-protective exorcism by the Temple. This sacrificial practice, and this transactionalism, rather than the corrupt venality of money-changing and commercial dealing practised in the outer court of the Temple, is what most deeply angers Jesus. That is the 'foundational thing' that the Cross addresses and it is what the Resurrection replaces.

That climactic outcome – here is Girard's decisive and perhaps most brilliant insight – is anticipated and triggered directly in the slow-burning confrontation of the Gospels with the scribes and Pharisees, who are challenged as deniers and would-be murderers of the good and holy God, whose Kingdom Jesus proclaims and embodies.

Clearly enough, the proclamation of God's Kingdom takes on a newly radical form in response to the growing resistance it encounters in the teaching, preaching and healing ministry of Jesus; but what is it, specifically, that triggers that very definite focussing, evinced by the Gospel narratives, towards the outcome of an exemplary death by crucifixion in Jerusalem? 'And I, when I am lifted up from the earth, will draw all men to myself' (John 12:32). We may think that this declaration of intent made by Jesus in St John's gospel, at the beginning of Holy Week, comes closest to gathering up the intentional movement of the teaching and healing ministry together with the Cross, in one single weave. It brings into focus the central question: what is the logic and the necessity of his own sacrificial death?

Girard spells out, originally and, I think, profoundly, the most Christian answer: it is the clear intelligence shown by Jesus of the phenomenon of founding murder. And the evidence for this claim? It lies, says René Girard, where we were most afraid to look for it, in what used to be called the 'cursing' of the scribes and Pharisees.

Political correctness, hard won and necessary, makes us, today, shy away from these potent and searing indictments. However, they are crucial. They point to the very things said by Jesus to be 'hidden since the foundation of the world'.

This idea is already present in Matthew 23:27-36:

> Woe to you, scribes and Pharisees, hypocrites. For you are like whitewashed tombs, which on the outside look beautiful, but inside they are full of the bones of the dead and of all kinds of filth. So you also on the outside look righteous to others, but inside you are full of hypocrisy and lawlessness. . . . Thus you testify against yourselves that you are descendants of those who murdered the prophets. Fill up the measure of your ancestors . . . so that upon you may come all the righteous blood shed on earth, from the blood of righteous Abel to the blood of Zechariah, . . . whom you murdered between the sanctuary and the altar. Truly I tell you, all this will come upon this generation'.

In Luke's gospel, the universal dimension of the drama of concealed sacral violence is highlighted by the charge that the Pharisees have 'taken away the key to knowledge' (Luke 11:52). Moreover, the equivalent passage in Luke (11:47-52), significantly, precedes the lament over Jerusalem and the expression used is 'from the foundation of the world': *'apo kataboles kosmou'* (v. 50). Let's be clear, says Girard: this cannot designate the same beginning, the same inaugural setting up, as the one we encounter in the prologue of John, where a different word is used (*en arche estin ho logos*). Luke's expression refers to the life of this earth; it refers to the founding of the world of human culture and society. That same solemn expression is echoed in Matthew 13:35, in which Jesus applies – at that point, to his own teaching, rather than to his Passion – the expression borrowed from Psalm 78: 'I will proclaim what has been hidden since the foundation of the world' (cf. also John 8:43-44).

We can see in the passage just quoted that Jesus foresees his own death (as the last of the prophets and as Messiah) and that he places it in direct line of descent from the murders committed by the leaders of theocratic Israel against the righteous, starting, significantly from Cain's victim, Abel. Indeed, it may be that this very searing challenge to the religious establishment ('fill up the measure of your ancestors!') itself triggers the resolution of the religious leaders to seek his death.

In John's gospel (8: 43-44) that confrontational trigger is even clearer and it is even more radically identified. Jesus indicts the religious leaders of Israel of spiritual solidarity with Satan, the father of murder and lies, of self-mystifying duplicity and the violent cover-up of murder. Girard says: 'John's text goes further than the others in disentangling the founding mechanisms; it excises all the definitions and specifications that might bring about a mythic interpretation. . . . Satan denotes the founding mechanism itself – the principle of all human community' (*TH* 1987: 161-62. See also *S* 1986: 184-97)). That same indictment embraces – in John (alone) it does so from the beginning of the ministry of Jesus – the cleansing of the Temple. The expression we like to remember from the Synoptics about 'my Father's house' being made into a 'den of thieves' is not just about the venality of the sacrificial system, it's about the twice-daily bloodbath of substitutionary animal sacrifice and all the religious transactionalism, evasion, hypocrisy and double-think developing out of it (we remember Matthew's expression 'all manner of filth').

We have to consider, therefore, that the polemic in relation to the Temple is not really about simony; it is, in its ultimate dimension, a searching challenge reaching down towards the tangled and entangled roots of violence and the sacred.

Jesus is saying: the Jewish religious leaders are blocking the coming of God's Kingdom; and they are doing so because they see, judge and react in the logic of the archaic sacred. Moreover, he reveals the non-visible and inavowable foundation – the underlying reality of the 'decomposing corpse', in concealment of which, those honorific and memorialising tombs to the prophets have been erected.

That unveiling, that opening up of the grave of human misrecognition and unknowing, that disclosure of the reality of founding murder, is the operative factor that seals his fate. It is, exactly speaking, intolerable. For that accusation, subverting the authority and standing of Israel's leaders utterly, Jesus must be done away with, albeit under legitimising headings of transferred blame – 'irreligion', 'blasphemy', 'danger to national security'.

Of course, alarm bells will, at this point, be ringing loudly in our modern ears. Are we too, in turn, about to scapegoat the entire tradition of historic Israel; are we engaging in a counter-transfer of blame, this time racially motivated? Isn't that what mediaeval Christendom did, indeed, actually come to? What some Christians are still capable of?

In answer to those latter two aberrations, it is indeed so – alas, yes. But, 'No', replies Girard firmly, '*not so* in respect of Israel as such; *not so* in the gospels'.[8] If the indictment is understood exactly, the formula used by Jesus should be, on the contrary, reconciling – even, eventually, therapeutic in the context of Jewish-Christian relations and then very much more widely – because it points to the common human mechanisms of violence and the sacred at work as much in the Shoah as in the Passion of the Christ.

Certainly, this drama of hidden things is being played out, where – to Israel's immense credit and eternal honour – it could only be played out: i.e. within Israel. However, all humanity, by virtue of its evolutionary formation, thanks to the very process of biological speciation producing homo sapiens, is programmed by, and embedded in, the default mechanism of group survival by emissary victimisation; and is consequently imprinted with the logic of founding murder.[9]

Israel's leaders are not, that is to say, being indicted anti-semitically, as Jews. Rather, they are being indicted by a fellow Jew, for a strategic and crucial deficit of authentically justifying Judaity. The whole point being made by Jesus is that they are, within Judaism, acting *de facto* as spokesmen for the archaic sacred, reinforcing and recycling its self-mystifying misrecognition (*TH* 1987: 164). It is that, by this stance, they are barring the way to what the prophetic tradition within Israel has already foreseen as the authentic coming of God's Kingdom. Ignoring God's salvation, come among men and even now at hand, they are playing instead for national survival in a scenario of founding murder.

* * *

That thought deserves some due space of resonance. 'Religion is organised around a more or less violent disavowal of human violence', so says Girard in *Things Hidden* (1987: 166). He adds immediately: 'that is what the religion that comes from men amounts to, as opposed to the religion that comes from God'. However, the resonance of what Girard explains in principle and shows at work, very precisely, in the Gospels,

---

8. See 'The Question of Anti-semitism in the Gospels' (Williams 1996: 211-21).
9. The motif of the tomb is integral to the meaning of this Gospel episode (as also, later, to the burial and Resurrection of Jesus). For Girard, tombs are the first evidences of culture; and culture develops as a form of extended tomb, since everything is built up around the transfiguringly sacralised and concealed death of the emissary victim, which provides, subterraneously, a secret influx of life (cf. *TH* 83).

has, of course, been heard elsewhere. 'Men never do evil so completely and cheerfully as when they do it as a matter of conscience (Pensée no. 895 in my Brunschvicg edition - Pascal, *Pensés et Opuscules*, ed. Léon Brunschvicg, Paris, Hachette, 1959, p.739). 'The historical religions have a tendency to become ends in themselves and, as it were, to put themselves in God's place; and, in fact, there is nothing that is so apt to obscure the face of God as a religion' (Jewish philosopher and theologian, Martin Buber).[10]

Can we, in turn, agree to agree with these thinkers? And with the Jesus of the gospels, who first formulates this insight decisively and crucially? Can we even extend our gratitude for recognising this fact-made-manifest to René Girard, who offers to help us see how that scandal comes to be and how it plays out in historical time? Why, in the first place, there is a buried scandal; why recognition of it challenges only those human things that should be challenged; and why, in an evolutionary world and an emergent Creation, the challenge made is always pertinent?

If so, the path is clear to understanding the intentionality of the Cross and its foreseeable effects: 'Now is the judgment of this world'. And of Israel? --Yes, of Israel too but as the pioneering paradigm of everybody else. 'Now is the ruler of this world cast out. And I, when I am lifted up from the earth, will draw *all men* to myself' (John 12: 31-32).

We have now reached the heart of the problem of violence and the sacred. The pivotal point, perhaps, from which the enterprise of Reconciliation can begin to find its vocation, its voice and its way.

---

10. The latter two sayings are popularised online as 'Quotes from the Philosophers'. The exact form of each is in dispute. Pascal is misquoted here, and often elsewhere, as saying 'from religious conviction'. Buber is translated freely or paraphrased in the form: 'Nothing so tends to mask the face of God as religion; it can be a substitute for God Himself.' See https:/www.azquotes.com./quote/225758 and www.azquotes.com/quote/ 1467913.

5
Passion, Resurrection – and How We Come by Reconciliation

Religion – but let us now say, lest we simplify, distort and falsify everything we most wish to understand: first-form or archaic-sacral religion – is born out of violence sacralised, covered up by lying, self-mystification and further violence. 'I will utter things hidden from the foundation of the world' (Matthew 13:35): the scribes and Pharisees of Jesus' time are embedded, as we all are, in a logic of founding murder, the dynamics of which, in Girard's very original submission, are fully transparent to Jesus. This group is indicted by Jesus in the Gospels, not anti-semitically, but for their role as a religious authority speaking out of the archaic sacred and itself pursuing a course of founding murder.

To make this – literally crucial – point so economically and so cogently is a signature achievement of Girard's theory. However, by way of giving proper relief and shading to the similarities and dissimilarities we need to highlight, it will be useful to introduce here a parallel case which displays a similar archaic-sacral pattern and is non-Jewish. It will be helpful to say that the Jewish leaders follow this pattern no less surely than the Druid priests who, in Celtic Ireland, just a little earlier in human history, killed Croghan Man.[1]

Who or what is Croghan Man? He is (for us) an example of archaic-sacral sacrifice but, before that, he is an amazingly well-preserved corpse, found buried in a bog on the outskirts of an ancient settlement in County Offaly, not far from present-day Dublin, in Ireland, in a site of which the 'king-making hill' is the sacred centre.

---

1. This case was investigated in a TV documentary 'Mummies Alive', shown by the Channel *Yesterday*, at 14.00, Thurs. 10 March, 2016.

The bog-preserved corpse has been dated to the period 400-200 BCE and is one of a number of similarly preserved corpses dating from that period. His physique, his diet, his clothing indicate he was a king. The king, in that time and place, was chosen to represent his people vis-à-vis cosmic powers (i.e. he was a sacred mediator); his role was to procure their favour, thereby securing the survival and flourishing of his people. Accordingly, the king was ritually married to the earth goddess and thus rendered responsible for weather, fruitfulness of the land (i.e. food supply) and of human fertility (i.e. community survival).

This particular bog-buried king, it is clear, died a violent, ritual death. He seems to have been accompanied in procession into the bog and there killed by four axe blows to skull and face, any one of which would have been enough to kill him. He also bears a signature wound: the excision of the left nipple. From Saint Patrick himself, we learn later that, in early Druidic Ireland, 'suckling from the king's nipple' was a metaphor for acknowledging subject dependency or pledging allegiance. It is reasonable to suppose that the excision symbolised some sort of revocation of kingly function, possibly following some form of judicial process.

He was ritually killed (sacrificed) by Druid priests when it became apparent, politically speaking, that he was not 'doing the job' and that another, younger, sacral king had to be tried. Remains of his stomach contents show that he had a last ritual meal of corn and buttermilk – a 'last supper' reminiscent of his function. His death outside the settlement boundary is symmetrical to his marriage at the ritual or sacred centre (not yet a temple).

Immediate scanning of the comparison suggests that a number of things present in the gospels were not, or were less, present in the case of Croghan Man (which is, of course, scripturally unrecorded). The sacrificial victim was buried in the bog, and that was the end of it. There was no return, no resurrection; except, conceivably, in the Girardian scenario whereby the victim is, in the telling of his story, sacralised as divine messenger. We do not know how the good news was conveyed by the priests to the people. Clearly, however, no memorial tombs were required to persuade them; and we have no reason to think that the justice, truthfulness and authority of the priestly class itself was in any way challenged; or that anyone thought to question whether the sacrificial victim was guilty as charged (i.e. was actually responsible for the weather, the bad harvest or the falling birth-rate).

Despite predictable dissimilarities of time and place, Croghan Man offers a *prima facie* parallel between two cases of archaic-sacral behaviour. Nevertheless, as we already begin to see, the same case can also help us contrast two models of sacrifice (archaic-sacral and Christian) that we all normally conflate and confuse for want of understanding their genesis and development in historical time.

* * *

Once we have processed the very striking account he gives us of the hinterland in the gospels of the Passion of Jesus, Girard is able to show us how every aspect of the Passion itself represents a deliberate, exemplary, almost pedagogic replay of the scenario of founding murder.

This is strikingly clear in the conspiracy to get rid of Jesus by the leaders of the Sanhedrin: 'It is better for you to have one man die for the people than to have the whole nation destroyed' (John 11:50). Caiaphas gives us here the exact, recapitulative formula of the victimary mechanism in action; he declares cynically, invoking a long-practised *raison d'état*, the scapegoating logic of blood-sacrifice as taken up into the cultural bloodstream of humanity. Clearly, Caiaphas fears the clouds of apocalypse gathering once more above Israel (cf. Luke 13:1 on the immediately preceding case of insurgency by the Galileans whose blood Pilate had 'mingled with their sacrifices'). This fear mirrors the pattern declared, so Jesus has told the chief priests and elders, throughout Israel's history.[2]

The tragic irony is that killing one more prophet, this one the Messiah of God, won't save the nation from the apocalypse of man-made destruction which, already, very perceptibly, looms over Israel. The parable of the corrupt tenants (or 'wicked husbandmen') becomes luminously clear when read as a vehicle for a coded warning of this eventuality; and Luke 11:49-50 is a commentary developing the same message in plain speech.

Jesus is not simply the victim of a conspiracy to murder, nor is he merely betrayed to that conspiracy from within, by one of his own. His actual death warrant is signed – in a juridical sense, which is crucial – by the Procurator of the occupying power, Pontius Pilate, albeit, with a

---

2. Girard's commentary has already stressed the link between this politico-religious crisis and all the previous crises of Israel's history. Caiaphas' advice to the Sanhedrin makes him, in effect, the depository of the sacrificial system as such: 'The scapegoat effect coming together before our eyes is the same as the scapegoat effect at the origin of Jewish [Temple] sacrifices. Caiaphas is the perfect Sacrificer, someone who puts victims to death in order to save the living' (S 1986: 114).

significant complication. At the level of brutal street politics, Pilate finds it expedient to re-activate, within the due process of Roman law, a more primitive reality. In the endgame, played out in what Christians have come to call Holy Week, Jesus is done to death by popular acclamation. What we observe here is the all-against-one of the most primitive mimetic crisis and the contagion of blood-fever in the re-gathered first diaspora of Israel – its Gentile observers and international travellers being, no doubt, also swept along.

The aspect of collective lynching is, in the last resort, decisive; its persuasion so potent that it takes over even the 'Hosanna!' crowds of a few days previously; reversing the acclamation of the triumphal entry into Jerusalem (Matthew 21:3-11; Mark 11:1-11; Luke 19:28-44; John 12:2-19). Conspicuously, in an ultimate test of potency, it overtakes and it takes over, in their denial and flight, the pledged, practised and forewarned loyalty of the disciples of Jesus (a spectacular confirmation, says, Girard, of the all-powerful scapegoating persuasion of the collective persecutory representation [S 1986: 105]).

What is founding in humanity is here declared to be something to which we can, all of us, in times of supreme crisis, regress. Observe the scene of mimetic rivalry, rage and deflected responsibility played out between Pilate and crowd. Pilate, relaying Caiaphas, is in effect asking – this is a deep irony, echoing Leviticus 16 – which scapegoat is it to be? The choice is between the malodorous goat Barabbas (Barabbas of the blood-stained sword, of the sacralised national cause, nobly covering a practice of greed, robbery and bloody murder: truly, therefore, a figure of violent archaic sacrality) and Jesus, innocent Lamb of God (see S 1986: 117). A single emissary victim is designated by rage-modelling leaders planted by the High Priest within the crowd; a fever of blood-lust sweeps over all. They need to be safe in the storm, they need to be innocent, to deflect guilt and avoid pain and catastrophe, at someone else's expense.

Vox populi, vox dei: the voice that speaks here is that of the collective god of the archaic sacred and his wrathful thunder is terrifying. Mark records (14:51-52) how one young follower – possibly even himself, evoked anonymously for the very shame of it – ran away naked, i.e. denuded of all defences against that archaic sacral dread we first observed, it will be remembered, in the passage from *Lord of the Flies*. Jesus is sentenced to death by acclamation; an acclamation rising to a crescendo, chanting a blood-beat slogan that sends us straight back to the climactic scene of mimetic crisis in that novel: 'Kill the Beast, kill the Beast!', 'Crucify him, crucify him!'

The contagion of victimary rage is present again in the derision and cursing of bystanders of the crucifixion. Even the cursing thief on his cross is a mimetic echo of the 'all-against-one'. More obliquely, the same can be said of the mock-obeisance of the soldiers and the subsequent scourging (Mark 15:16-19; John 19:1-3). In the classic work of Victorian anthropology, *The Golden Bough*, Sir James Frazer noted strange precedents in world religious mythologies: victims becoming kings, kings becoming victims; and we are in a position to add here that the death of Croghan Man presents one more allusive echo of this type. However, Girard answers Frazer's reductionism: 'Because it reproduces the founding event of all rituals, the Passion is connected with every ritual on the entire planet' (*TH* 1987: 167).

Nor must we forget the modality of this execution: death by crucifixion. That particular instrument of judicial process and political power was reserved for slaves and foreign enemies of the state; it was a special death of ignominy and rejection, performed outside the city walls. It takes that form because it is a signature act of founding murder, as required by the sacral bond itself. It represents an institutionalised politico-legal development of the very first binding and bonding rite: archaic blood-sacrifice. Is it not suggestive, if we look back to the pillars demarcating the sacred and sacrificial space at the centre of the world's oldest temple at Göbekli Tepe, that they bear a distinct T-shape, anticipating the original first-shape taken in a number of Mediterranean countries by the cross of crucifixion?

Seven or eight thousand years later, the cross has assumed the shape now known to us; and, for imperial Rome, it has become a judicial instrument and a political institution. It says: defy the most sacred thing there is – Roman state power – and you'll wind up here, like this . . . Exhibited, that is, in a grim pedagogy of derision and deterrence; slowly and remorselessly disarticulated, stripped of all dignity, of all capacities and attributes of human subjecthood, and, at agonising length, of life itself.

As we come to realise that the entire scenario of the Passion is, in sum and recapitulatively, a replay of the archetypal scenario of founding murder, we acquire a powerful new insight into that very mysterious thing, the intentionality of the Cross. Now we can begin to see what it was (if we are Christians, we may add: *and is*) in the mind of the Subject who conceives and executes it – freely, lucidly, in a strange resolution of consent and obedience.

Jesus consents to enter into the scenario of founding murder as victim in order to display that process at work in his people and in humankind and to reveal to all humans its nothingness in relation to the ultimate reality of the love of God. In other words, this strange project aims to rework the deepest and darkest springs of perverted proto-sacrality and of sacralised violence in the human heart, to change its very mainspring of desire; and, thus to convert those in whom this darkness operates (which is to say, all human beings) to the reality of the Kingdom-that-comes. Here is an antipodal pedagogy, reversing the grim pedagogy of fear, expiation and deterrence – here is a strange therapy of love.

At one level, therefore, we must see Jesus as a scapegoat victim of human violence like any other. Girard declares explicitly that there is nothing unique, or even unusual, in the malefic or malignant dimension of this crucifixion, only, he insists, in its work of redemptive revelation (S 1986: 111), which concerns its dimension of goodness and love: 'There is only one transcendence in the Gospels, that of the love divine which triumphs over all manifestations of violence and the sacred by revealing their nothingness' (S 1986: 194).

Is Girard then saying as some 'Inspector Clouseau' style British commentators have repeatedly claimed, usually amid flourishes of rhetorical indignation, that this reprised scenario simply repeats the founding murder? Exactly and pointedly not. Between the old and the new structure, 'there is a radical, an abyss-like [Fr. '*abyssale*'] opposition' (*TH* 1987: 217).[3] It is, deliberately, the same scenario but turned upside down and run backwards in order that it be recognised, disarmed, undone, defeated.

What, exactly, does the inverting and the converting? For Girard, it is the undeniable innocence (or goodness) of this victim. This is what causes the default mechanism of unanimous condemnation, hence, also, in consequence, the entire machine of archaic-sacral mystification and cover-up, to malfunction. No, if we look again, there is not, in this scapegoat murder, save fleetingly, at the apex point of the mimetic crisis, a flawless unanimity. Pilate, in his rational and equitable moment, has already seen through the charges laid against his victim (Matthew 27:24; Mark 15:14; Luke 23:4; John 18:38). When he aligns himself with the crowd, his wife intervenes urgently, if vainly, to protect this innocent from capital execution (Matthew 27:18; cf. *S* 1986: 106-7). In Luke, the penitent thief answers the cursing thief: 'this man has done nothing wrong' (Luke 23:41); and in Mark, even the executing centurion's verdict is that this was a just man, in the image of God (Mark 15:39).

---

3. I have amended the poor English translation, which renders Fr. '*abyssale*' by Eng. 'abysmal'.

Then, the inverse or antithetical sense of this victimary scenario is consecrated – not *post factum* by public opinion – but in advance, by the victim himself, steadfast in purpose, assured of his vindication by God and by history. The Last Supper deliberately reprises the Jewish Passover meal but also, behind that very deliberate allusion and the continuity it establishes with Jewish tradition, way back upstream in time, it re-enacts and rewrites the festive meal that originally precedes – it does so, for instance, both at Göbekli Tepe and in the case of Croghan man – the archaic sacrifice itself.

Archbishop Michael Ramsey used to delight in saying: 'The Cross is not a defeat which requires the Resurrection to reverse it. Of itself, the Cross is already a victory.' Yes, a victory for the victim, who declares himself, paradoxically, the actively directing Subject: even of this death, designed, in principle, to harrow and disintegrate the human subject as such. It is also true that the Resurrection experiences of encounter confirm his pioneering and paradoxical confidence. They add a swelling tide of new and freshly motivated counter-conviction by allowing his victory to be known and by declaring its newly foundational vigour.

The bodily Resurrection of the scapegoat victim is, of course, the other new thing – the feature that, conspicuously, does not figure in the original model of founding murder. Girard, as anthropologist of the religious dimension in humankind, cannot and will not speak about this event theologically. He does not say, for instance, with all traditional theologians, that the Resurrection is the ultimate divine vindication of Israel's Messiah; nor (as traditional theologians might well agree) does he call it the ultimate effect of the theological mimesis between Father and Son, to which Jesus himself, in John's account, draws attention; nor does he say that the utterly unexpected reappearance, in the middle of history, of the bodily resurrected Son of Man, represents a dramatically counter-cultural preview of the divinely purposed end-time of history and of Creation (Wright 2007: 103ff.). He does not even say that all of Jesus' Gospel miracles have just that dimension of vertical mimesis and realised eschatology (Lewis 1976: 99ff). No, René Girard, who, indeed, personally – so I would judge from having known him – was entirely disposed to accept all these affirmations, nevertheless looked to his theologian colleagues to spell out what are, of course, theological implications and assertions. (This makes some theologians nervous: 'But why aren't you agreeing with us; why aren't you confirming what we say, in the way we say it? Why this deficit, this defection?')[4]

4. The frustrations experienced by the theologian in this dialogue with R.G. are

Nonetheless, Girard reads pertinently the great bow-wave of the Resurrection. He sees it as being exactly what the Gospel writers present it as being but this phenomenon is read, in his formulation, anthropologically. He points out, for instance, that the Resurrection is that which surprises all the actors, which throws into reverse gear and eventually overthrows the mimetic process of sacralisation and of self-mystification. So that, not only does the scapegoat's condemnation not stick, not only is the scapegoaters' hatred exposed for what it is ('They hated me without a cause', John 15: 25; cf. Psalm 35:19; S 1986:102-03), but the entire enfolded-enfolding logic of emissary victimisation and scapegoat violence, diffused throughout all human cultures, is, for the first time, pierced through and fully laid bare. What is finally nailed by it is the unknowing – but also self-deceiving and secretly complicitous – human self-misrecognition.

This anthropological focus notwithstanding, Girard, in strict logical solidarity, sees also a new revelation of the nature of God: '[This] is no longer men fabricating gods, it is God who has come to take the place of the victim. . . . This victim is divine before any sacralisation. The divine precedes its sacralisation [i.e. it does not proceed from it]. The rights of God are re-established' (*BE* 2010: 109). There we can see the link between the foundation recalled by the Cross and that other, even more foundational beginning proclaimed in John's gospel: 'In the beginning was the Word.' In order to designate the logic of founding murder in which humanity, as a whole and aboriginally, is embedded, and to be 'raised' after doing so, the one who bears witness to the truth must, in all rigour, have transcended that logic and stand in that truth; he must have been enacting a higher identity, a prior calling (cf. *TH* 1987: 215-220 on the 'Divinity of Christ').

The exact Girardian formulation, therefore, is this: 'In a way, it is because Christ entered into the mould of false resurrections ['*est entré dans le moule des résurrections fausses*'] that he is truly risen' (*BE* 2010: xvi). Exactly so; as Croghan Man is not. Only someone who, going where everyone goes, yet sharing that other identity, that other, prior beginning, can designate with such accuracy the evolutionary archetype and disarm human self-misrecognition; only such a one can break its

---

understandable too, for instance, when R.G. writes: 'The essential thing about the revelation, from an anthropological viewpoint, is the crisis it provokes in every representation of persecution from the standpoint of the persecutor'(*S* 1986: 114). One imagines the dialogue: 'Fine. So how does that revelation advance Revelation? Can you tell us more about that?' 'Ah, well, I was rather thinking that was your job?'

hold over humankind in principle. The Cross is both that awesome mirror held up in judgement to the self-sacralising violence of man and a direct epiphany of the transcendent love by and from whom that light proceeds. The Resurrection says: the auto-generated binding spell is forever broken.

That is also clear when Girard comments on the words of the crucified Jesus: 'They know not what they do.' These words, says Girard, must, pace Freud, be accounted as the first and most decisive declaration of the unconscious in human history (*S* 1986: 111). For the first time, humankind is delivered from its imprisonment in the archaic dreamsphere of self-deceiving mythic falsehood. However, it is also true that Jesus, Son of God, alone and uniquely, can say '*They know not what they do.*' This forgiving victim is unique and, as such, he mediates something unique from his heavenly Father to humankind – the transforming gift of leaving the company of them (the victimisers) and entering into the life of us (the love replicated in mutual exchange between Father and Son) which is what communicates across that divide: the understanding of forgiving love itself and the grace of sharing in its novel empowerment.

It is striking and noteworthy that the risen – hence restored, vindicated, newly empowered – Christ remains totally in the role of forgiving victim. Thus, his first greeting to his disloyal disciples is one of 'Peace!' (not of condemnation or reproach). More eloquently still, he slips past their very telling invitation, 'Lord, are you at this time going to restore the Kingdom to Israel?' (Acts 1:6), and evades their stubbornly persistent expectation that he will wish to reverse his popular rejection and be revenged for his condemnation by the political and religious establishment of his nation. It is also true that this conspicuous lack of any vindictive or punitive intent stands in direct continuity with his last apocalyptic warnings (in the synoptic Gospels) about the politico-cosmic turmoil still to come upon Israel. These are warnings against the times, in which looms the destruction of Israel's Temple, and they come with expressions of deepest compassion for the victims of such times and an urgent invitation to his disciples to remain watchful and steadfastly committed to what God is accomplishing despite and through such bitter turmoil (*TH* 1987: 202-5).

This unveiling of the hidden truth about humankind, including its most foundational illusion as to the virtue of blood-sacrifice as propitiation and exorcism, Girard insists, has been, is now, and will be in historical culture-time, world-changing:

> By putting Jesus to death, the powers actually fall into a sort of trap, which lets slip their all-time secret. . . . The scapegoat mechanism emerges into the most illuminating of all lights; it becomes subject to the most intense publicity, and the best known thing in the world. It is out of this knowledge that humankind will learn, slowly, very slowly . . . to slip underneath the persecutory representation of violence. (S 1986: 108)

Where the world's religious mythologies were universally complicit in the mystifying cover-up of humankind's enfoldment within violence, the Gospels represent the archaic-sacral mystification machine working at full tilt and, for the first time, failing to carry the verdict of history; and they enable us, in its represented failure, to deconstruct the very mechanisms of religious authority, political power, mystified sacred rage, social advantage and double-think that allow the system, as such, to function below the line, subterraneously.

Girard thus speaks of 'this extraordinary work of the gospels: persecutory representation abrogated, broken, revoked' (S 1986: 103); 'By submitting to violence, Christ reveals and uproots the structural matrix of all religion' (TH 1987: 178-79). The gospels, on this reading, declare the very thing that, historically, has made – and still makes – 'archaic religion' archaic.

In the last analysis, then, we may say that Girard's novel and transforming figure of sense is this: Jesus, knowing intimately the fact and the logic of founding murder, consents to enter into it and assume it self-sacrificially – as victim. The love divine must, in the end, itself suffer in full the most extreme worldly consequences of human violence, in order that the lie at the heart of the archaic sacred be ultimately nailed – the lie about the innocence of man, functioning in complicitous reciprocity with the lie about the vengeful and punitive interventionism of God. Only so can the very spring and principle of blood sacrifice, enfolded deep into all human works and systems – and, even before that afforded a permitted place within a free, self-organising creation – be reworked into a triumph of love. Only so does the mimetic creature have an adequate model for positive mimesis. Only so does the new communion, the ecclesial community of God-with-us, come to a new and adequate foundation.

Perhaps we can now see why Girard's last work of religious commentary takes its title from a little known and strangely unfamiliar saying in Luke's gospel (10:18): 'I see Satan fall like lightning' (1999 in French; 2001 for the English translation). Jesus welcomes back the 70 disciples sent out on a mission of proclamation of God's Kingdom and healing. He learns of their power to reproduce – this is Spirit-empowered mimesis! – his own miracles of healing and exorcism. Here, therefore, is his exultant realisation that the grace of overcoming evil has passed from himself, bringer and bearer of the Kingdom, to those who follow him – Jesus at this point delivers this potent and jagged prophetic insight.

He sees the 'prince of this world' striking down in a lightning bolt of apocalyptic devastation from a turbulent and violent heaven; but thereby also falling to earth, undone in the very act of his ascendancy, stripped of his sacralised prestige, and broken in his power over God's creation. That, he foresees, is how the Light will get in; that is how the epiphany of the truth of the loving kindness and mercy of God will shine through and gain traction in a world of evolutionary survival (as we would today call it) and human freedom.

John says the same thing as Luke, rather more theologically: 'Now is the judgment of this world. Now is the ruler of this world cast out. And I, when I am lifted up from the earth will draw all men to myself' (John 12:31-32). From the greatest peril will be crafted the supreme opportunity. From the poison itself the antidote will be drawn. The Christ himself must take the hit for man's ersatz transcendence – the apocalypse of human wrath masquerading as divinity, invoking divine sanction and inspiration (i.e. projected onto God). He must proclaim the 'things hidden since the foundation of the world'.

If – and as – we come to grasp that remarkable figure of sense, we will be able to see also that the Cross of Christ already, amid all the world's evils, also has Islamic State in view. We might almost say: it has in view IS as a recapitulative figure of all the world's ills; and, arriving at this recognition, we begin to measure the theological centrality of Girard's long anthropological argument.

Looking with René Girard, over the shoulder of the Son of Man, the burning persuasion born in the disciples on the Emmaus road springs at once into focus, clear strategically, in its temporal depth: from Cain, who shed the blood of innocent Abel, via the rejection of many prophets, to the most recent murder of John the Baptist by Herod, and now of Jesus by . . . well, everybody. That clears the screen of our seeing in a newly strategic and very radical way; it renews our scanning of revelation through the scriptures; so that, in newly positive (good) mimetic reciprocity, we begin to discern the contrapuntal theme of divine deliverance, salvation.

We can see how the story of God's Messiah – from the binding of Isaac, the scapegoating expiation of Leviticus 16, the innocent affliction of Job, through the suffering servant of Deutero-Isaiah, right through to the Cross – is the story of the reversal of sacred violence, and the rewriting of archaic-sacral sacrifice by the transforming operation of the perfectly altruistic, self-giving, faith-enlivening, Creation-pursuing love divine.

Archaic-sacral sacrifice has, in the process we have been following, taken on a reversed (i.e. an inverse and antipodal) form, a form imprinting into the old word (which our language retains, often still freighted with its first sense) a new meaning and concept. From bloody immolation of scapegoat victim (that definition is still entirely valid for Croghan Man), the same word has acquired a new semantic content, antipodally different from its original meaning. The new second sense is perfectly altruistic and God-shaped self-offering, exactly mirroring the love divine. The new Christic pattern is, in the divine work which Christians have since come to see in the Cross of Christ, superimposed on the archaic-sacral pattern expressed in the Roman practice of crucifixion.

The intention and effect of the Cross is to transform radically – not just the practice and institution of sacrifice – but, more strategically, the theme of salvation itself. It transforms *homo religiosus*, starting with the archaic man latent still in each one of us, then the sacrificial logic expressed covertly also in our communal and social life and in the programming set of references, memories and values which inform the common mental space within which our social life is enacted (that is to say, broadly speaking, our culture).

Retold by the risen Christ, here is the inside track on how God was then and is, even now, as Saint Paul says, 'reconciling the world to himself' (2 Corinthians 5:18), thus bringing to fulfilment the Abrahamic promise of blessing upon all nations.

If there were world enough and time, we might go on to explore that same inside track systematically. We might hope to do so by showing how Girard's very central understanding unlocks, first of all, the faithfully replicated new sacrifice of love in the first martyr Stephen (*TH* 1987: 170-74), then the paradigmatic conversion of Saint Paul, archaic-sacral zealot converted by and to the new sacrifice of love – so much so that he speaks of the 'old man' being made anew, and the powers and principalities of the archaic sacred conquered (*TH* 1987: 192, 224, 252, 428).

We might see how it redefines the cloudy archaic-sacral notion of apocalypse; and how, finally, it re-evaluates all the various Christian theories of atonement, most of which are still hybrid theories, struggling to catch up with the radical transformation undergone by the concept of sacrifice in the Passion and Resurrection of Jesus (while succeeding, often enough, only just a little better than the archaic-sacral transactionalisms they claim to replace).

We might wish to work systematically through these confirmatory aspects and dimensions of Girard's key insights. It would be important to do so, if it is true, as Girard himself often claimed, that the value of a theory is to be judged by its power of consistent elucidation of problems and of data (natural scientists do not think or proceed otherwise). That would be to pursue the theme of how Christianity – as interpreted by Girard – makes newly accessible sense of the salvation of *homo religiosus*.

However, our own leading theme, focussed henceforth on our title 'Reconciliation', has an overriding claim. So, let us now, accordingly, cut to the chase.

* * *

We have, finally, to ask: what new and fruitful platform of intelligent thinking does the Girardian reading of Passion and Resurrection bring to the enterprise of reconciliation? What does Girardian theory, more generally, add to what is already established, understood and – sometimes, patchily and partially – practised under this name and in this field? Where does its singular advantage lie, its special focus and impetus?

Reconciliation is the process of bringing back into amity – or, at least, into some form of liveable and healing Other-reciprocity – relations that are broken or strained by misunderstanding, rivalry and conflict and, particularly, by violence. It is the art of healing the gaps, the knots, the bitter places, the black holes of mutual misunderstanding and enmity between persons and – this is increasingly crucial given the cultural development of humankind – between collectivities of persons (societies, cultures, nations, faiths), making peace between humans[5], between humans and their planetary home and – if we follow

---

5. To date, it is the inter-individual dimension of the mission of Reconciliation that has best recognised the potential of Girardian theory. See eg Simon J. Taylor, *Imitation and Scapegoats. Pastoral Insights from the work of René Girard* (Cambridge: Grove, 2016).

Girard – first of all and in principle, between God the Reconciler whose initiative we copy (i.e. recognise, interiorise, respond to in reciprocity) and the non-divine, human Other.

The breadth and depth of reconciliation in its fullest Lenten sense is given in that word from Saint Paul: 'All this is from God, who reconciled us to Himself through Christ and gave us the ministry of reconciliation . . . God was in Christ reconciling *the world* to Himself, not counting their sins against them' (2 Corinthians 5:18-19). We see at once why Girard (had he known of it) would have rejoiced at Coventry Cathedral's own calling to the mission and ministry of reconciliation. This ministry is usually defined in terms of the words used by Provost Howard on confronting the blitzed and blackened ruin of the old Cathedral, which was destroyed, together with much of the city of Coventry, by German bombing in 1940: 'Father, forgive.'

These words, cited in this form, have been adopted ever since at Coventry as symbol, as icon, and, increasingly, as a brand logo for Coventry's entire ministry of reconciliation. They form the epigraph of the whole effort of Cathedral and diocese in promoting, sustaining and linking in a solidarity of thought, prayer and action, similar enterprises worldwide, all of them addressed to resolving the multifarious kinds of human division, conflict or estrangement.

Such efforts are undertaken, usually, out of pressing need, in many lands and, usually, they connote practical projects of Christian inspiration, though the interfaith dimension has in recent years emerged into significance. Commonly, such linking solidarities are concretised by the gifting of a material object, the Cross of Nails, forged out of nails taken from the blitzed ruin of Coventry's old Cathedral; this gift serving as a reminder of the context, the inspiration and the cost of the action of reconciliation envisaged. The byword 'Father, forgive' also forms the basis of prayers and liturgies of reconciliation.

One of the advantages of the omnipresent use this shortened or edited formulation of the utterance of the crucified Christ in Luke's gospel is that, dispensing with the specified object of divine forgiveness ('Father, forgive *them*'), it allows would-be human practitioners of the sacrifice of love to invoke the paradigmatic model, while bracketing the ever-looming, innately human mimetic competition for the desirable high ground.

As long as we invoke the Other's guilt (and by implication our own innocence), we confine ourselves within the dynamics of common-or-garden moralism. As Girard sees so acutely, we are still seeing and acting ultimately in the logic of negative or conflictual mimesis; in which event, we belong still to the age-old human bent for guilt-evasion, blame-shifting and metaphysical self-assertion.

Structurally, reconciliation involves and requires a conversion of desire and, ultimately, even a transformation of identity: it calls forth a novel choice of positive mimesis in the likeness of its originating model, the dying, forgiving and risen Christ. Both these structural requirements become fully possible, and are genuinely met, only as we ourselves come to speak from the position of the demystified and forgiving victim; as we come to acknowledge, from having ourselves first known and received something of it, the higher, transcending reality of forgiveness. 'Father, forgive' is, in this sense, a realistic pointer to what is involved spiritually in reconciliation. Girard would have understood the anthropological realism of this starting point; as he would have welcomed the reminder it gives of gracious and enabling empowerment from above.

Traditionally, in Christian thought and practice, reconciliation operates along two axes: one vertical, which concerns heaven and earth, God and us; the other horizontal, which relates to this-worldly relationships between individuals and groups, social classes and genders, nations or geo-political, economic or ideological groupings, between humans and their environmental or cosmic home, humans and the rest of the animal creation – even, conceivably, one day, between 'earthlings' and 'aliens'. The two axes are said to be reciprocal in the sense that each interacts with the other and varies with the other (in fact and in representation, for both good and ill).

What distinguishes a Christian practice of reconciliation is the insistence that the first axis is the key to unlocking the second, i.e. it gets more deeply to the root of the problem; and it releases and supports, in more effective actuality, its positive energies, thus realising better its potential for making peace out of disharmony, rivalry, conflict or violence. In Girardian terms it is better at converting bad mimesis (in which rivalrous, destructive, self-fascinating and auto-renewing attitudes and behaviours are recycled with interest) into good mimesis (positive, peace-building, Other-accepting and life-enhancing, also recycled with interest). It thrives and flourishes most fully when predicated on Spirit-led discernment and practised within the energy-field of light and grace from above.

What else is the entire Judaeo-Christian history of salvation but the story of that conversion? Christ comes 'in the fulness of time' but from the beginning, reconciliation is conceived and enterprised by God; hence, in a real (intentional) sense, the Lamb is slain 'from the foundation of the world'.

Yet, there is a paradox. This conversion operating in reconcilers does not mean that the Christian praxis is inconceivable, inimitable or otherwise disqualified outside the original faith-matrix of Christian orthodoxy. The example of the good Samaritan is there to remind us of this. Conversion can proceed from the created goodness of a natural heart; in which case, justification in the sight of God follows from it. Jesus gives us, as observable criterion of true godlikeness, mimetic empathy expressed in service to the victim and he does so deliberately, in order to confound the complacent self-righteousness of religious orthodoxy and establishment. The refounding of human identities, the metamorphosis of the self of desire are not limited, therefore, to those accredited by their formal confessional belonging, nor, consequently, are the interlocutors and partners of Christianly motivated reconciliation.

'Everyone on the side of truth listens to me' (John 18:37); as everyone of goodwill recognises the goodness of the good Samaritan – yes, we do copy that (indeed, the parables are long-term telecommunication devices for inviting recognition of divine models to be freely and authentically interiorised). If it were not so, could the light that – according to John's prologue, 'lightens every man' – actually 'shine on in the darkness'? There is a capacity for positive mimesis in everyone and the potential in everyone to switch mimetic polarities from negative to positive. This insight is foundational to the Kingdom of God. It comes from the one who also saw and knew that the refusal of the Kingdom by his hearers and followers must logically draw them into turning against him; so that this very rejection would finally bring about the choice of himself as emissary victim; which is the price he pays to achieve the self-betrayal of sacred violence, lured into declaring openly, to all seeing, its hidden game (*TH* 1987: 211, cf. 208-9, 291).

Reading Girard, we realise with something of an electric shock that mimesis is a concept of truly fabulous reach and still largely unfathomed significance; since it encompasses such paradoxes as the one just mentioned. Moreover, it encompasses equally pre-human phenomena (such as the seabed-mimicking camouflage manufactured by the subsiding octopus) and it reaches up to include the fully reciprocal and genuinely theological mimesis between Father and Son. The notion of mimesis, suitably orchestrated, is capable of following and fathoming what the French poet Paul Claudel would have called the 'great Octave of Creation'.

What, however, and more precisely, does Girard add? What difference does he make? The simplest way of expressing this is perhaps to say that he takes us directly to the heart of the human problem. We understand, for the first time, in the light of his anthropological theory, the long intertwining in human affairs of violence and the sacred; and, as we follow the gentle but powerful reshaping that proceeds in the Biblical narratives, we are equipped to identify and tackle directly the real challenges posed by these residually archaic and tangled human realities; both within ourselves and in our world.

Anthropologically, he gives us a new take on relationships and a broader, deeper perspective. One currently prominent example is the way in which the affluent developed world is squaring up to the problem of ever-increasing flows of migration from the less-developed world (in the case of Europe, from Africa, the Middle East and beyond; in the case of North America, from Central and South America). To date, the response of developed nations has been almost entirely self-protective. We have seen a dozen variations on the impulse to take our own country outside the fall-out zone of this invasion (variously, by sending them home, building fences or walls, reinforcing border controls, refusing to accept resettlement quotas, denying citizenship to the 'invaders' etc.). In short, our first response has been to take counter-measures against the symptoms, while thrusting away the entire iceberg of the underlying problem and out-sourcing – but, of course, we really mean off-loading – the mountainous weight of its resolution. With Girard's help, we read transparently the sacrificial logic of such large-scale collective behaviour.

Mimetic theory obliges us to take the real measure of the problem; it permits us to engage with it and so to mobilise accurately and adequately for its resolution. Not only does it explain the wars, the economic rivalries, the physical and spiritual violence from which the Third World refugees flee; but, more significantly, it understands the mimetic impulse to reach out for the same advantages which our globalising world imprints ever-more vividly and desirably in the minds of the have-nots. It thereby makes transparent the structural inevitability of the problem of migration: as a momentum-gathering, globally instanced, reaching-out of hands towards the same objects of desire; and it foretells soberly the crescendo towards paroxysm that our own moral evasion and inaction risk aiding and abetting. It tells us accurately that we must act (and where, when and how much). Not just casually, in sometime compassion or out of reasonable equity, but, more cogently, to escape general apocalypse.

At which point, we can begin to benefit also from the insight that what is mimetically induced can be mimetically reversed: by foregrounding our relation to the victim, by changing the structural dynamics of desire and by offering newly collaborative models of peace-and-prosperity building. Whether Europe needs a European army is debateable, whether it needs a European Peace Corps is not, once a clear mimetic reading of that situation is established.

After Girard (to echo Bernard Perret's recent title), the project of reconciliation is no longer in the position of trying to project the shapes and meanings of theology, from above, without mediation, onto human behaviour. We can accept that we no longer need to convert interlocutors-in-reconciliation to our own identity-perspectives and faith-values before we can begin to make peace with them. Conceptually and tactically speaking, therefore, we are no longer attempting, to construct a jumbo jet, with household tools, in a suburban garage. Even our motivating altruism, fitful as it may be, will know why it can no longer remain as parochial as it was. Girard ushers in, modestly, the overdue time of theology and anthropology working together, at peace and in fruitful complementarity.

He calls attention to other overdue things as well, to 'Christian feelings falsified, distorted and partially neutralised by the deep-reaching rootedness in us of that from which we believe ourselves to have been already delivered: [archaic-sacral] sacrifice' (*TH* 1987: 226). We think here, immediately, of the Crusades, of mediaeval witch-hunting and Jew-baiting, the legacy of which has afforded a toxically respectable cover for ideologies of minority persecution, racial hatred and mass murder (from Dreyfus to the Holocaust). Girard's anti-sacrificial reading bids fair to deconstruct, with life-giving effects, the fossilized culture shell of historic Christianity.

We think of imperial nation-state religions, so potent in putting on our side an archaic-sacral and tribal God, and hence in the making of World War I (and many others). In forcing us to recognise and confront the sacrificial archaisms to which Christian thought and action have so often been subterraneously mortgaged, Girard unlocks the reconciliatory potential of Christianity itself.

We begin to see also the many so-called 'Christian' theological positions and propositions which should properly be called out as fundamentalist, since these too attest the archaic foundations to which they revert; for instance, the atonement theory known as penal substitution, a theory which, viewed through a Girardian lens, looks to be arbitrary as substitution, archaically deformed as sacrifice and fundamentally misconceived as transaction ('Tis done, the great Transaction's done!').[6] Or again, we might instance divinely vengeful, world-ending notions of apocalypse, complete with the rapture of the elect, snatched *in extremis* out of this doomed world and thus saved from the supposedly sacred violence of the Wrath to come.

We may even ask, with Bernard Perret, whether the prevalence of sexual abuse in the ranks of the clergy of many churches is not one more symptom of an archaic-sacrificial form of behaviour, concealed and legitimised by a hyper-sacralisation of the priestly function itself, and all the more prevalent wherever there is also a rebound from, or even a resentful revenge taken for, a self-mortifying 'sacrifice' of sexuality itself.

This is an extremely incomplete list of Christian crimes, misdeeds and theologico-moral ambiguities, past and present, all of which have the common root that they are pickled in unnoticed residues of archaic sacrality (especially in the logic of archaic sacrifice). It is a purely indicative list (if it were not, it would fill too many volumes!). Of course, it is right and good to add that similar lists might *a fortiori* be established for all religions and all faiths; and that they will apply even more integrally to the moral, social and political tissue of common secular cultures as such. Girard's theory has, indeed, a 360-degree pertinence and critical applicability.

It is worth repeating, moreover, that the effect of Girard's theory as a whole is to transform ultimately – not just the practice and institution of sacrifice – but *homo religiosus* as such; that is, the archaic-sacral man latent still in each one of us and expressed, consequently, in our communal and social life and in the programming set of references, memories, intentions and values which inform the given (if always-evolving) psychic force-field within which our social life is enacted, simply speaking, our culture.

We readily understand from the many glimpses of sacrificial logic and negative mimesis we have come across in these pages that the ills scanned for are indeed so pervasive that Girard has been accused of transforming the founding complicity of violence and the sacred into a replacement form of original sin!

---

6. First line of an Evangelical hymn, popular in the Victorian period by Philip Doddridge and still published in 14 English-language hymnals. My opposition to its flawed theology should not be taken as suggesting that the hymn itself is bad, or its sense of undeserved grace false.

On this fruitfully debateable point, I offer some preliminary thoughts. It is true that there are striking passages in his work which might suggest that conclusion.[7] Yet I never heard René Girard make any such claim of identity in seminars or conferences; or declare that the Girardian concept could or should replace the theological one. He was, in truth, the last thinker likely to mix up concepts belonging to different axes of reference (one horizontal, referring to inter-human rivalries, the other vertical, relating to the pre-loaded shortfall of human response to divine calling). His distinction between the beginnings of the human world (*apo kataboles kosmou*) and the beginnings of Creation (*en arche*) seem to me decisive in this respect. (That is not the case for the parallel concept of Satan, which Girard unquestionably treats as a sacralised mythic entity standing for a reality better described by the self-organising play of mimetic desire. Satan is the 'subject of the system' of mimetic rivalry: the perverse, ever reversible, conjunction of model and obstacle.)

And yet, whatever the case of Girard's own understanding, it is clearly helpful in the domain of reconciliation to keep open the question of original sin. It would be entirely in order (may I venture to suggest?) to think of forms of negative mimesis as illustrating metonymically (i.e. we might agree, at least experimentally, to take the part for the whole) the semantic contour of the theological idea, thereby giving all at the table of reconciliation at least some useful access to the idea of original sin. This is a doctrine which is often seen to be in need of repair in its traditional (Augustinian) definition. As far as the great majority of our contemporaries are concerned, it is certainly deeply lost in the thickest mists of age-old culture and it is currently inoperative in the practice of reconciliation. On the other hand, the impotence of human beings to lift themselves out of the fatality of circular and cyclical violence (for instance) is a cogent truth apparent to anyone who listens to the news; as is the omnipresence of Other-fascinated rivalries, unstable love-hates and self-sacralising retaliations, inflicting insult, injury and death.

---

7. See, for instance, Appendix, p. 122, or *QCC* 1994: 171: 'The prologue of St John's gospel is a kind of inversion of Genesis showing that it isn't God who expels man, as the scene of the earthly paradise tells us, but that it is man expelling God. That, in my opinion is how we should define original sin.' See also *TH* 223: "If Christ alone is innocent, then Adam is not the only one to be guilty. All men share in this archetypal state of blame, but only to the extent that the chance of becoming free has been offered to them and they have let it slip away. We can say that this sin is indeed *original* but only becomes actual when knowledge about violence is placed at humanity's disposal'. [Amended translation].

Moreover, it is possible, following Jesus, to transform the delight we all have in detecting the mote in someone else's eye into a discovery of the beam in our own; and Girard's theory is precisely a superb toolset for doing something very much like that over a vast diversity of types of rivalrous and conflictual situations: affective and personal, professional, socio-political, economic, religious and interfaith, global-ecological etc., in each of which, a body of applied Girardian scanning and analysis already exists and is rapidly expanding.

The theologian, in short, can be multiply grateful to the mediating anthropologist who translates his language and his models intelligibly, creates a congenial dynamic of engagement, starting from 'where we all are', and defines a terrain of common recognition. Particularly when the same mediator also provides a simple, concrete, but almost infinitely flexible – and therefore always pertinent – 'grid' for identifying problems and scanning their active components (negative mimesis, runaway dynamic, sacrificial logic, misrecognition, the mimetic crisis with its contexts and periodicities etc.). Still more so when the scanning of the problems suggests a counter-dynamic of transformation (simple in principle, fruitful in practice and variously applicable), namely, the transformation (metamorphosis, conversion) of bad (negative, hate-generating) into good (positive, loving) mimesis.

We can see also why Girard's theory is comprehensible to, and appeals to, people of all faiths and none. A Japanese linguist and culture-theorist comes to realise in dialogue with Girard that the word scapegoat is untranslateable in Japanese, since his culture is entirely embedded in the never-challenged legitimacy of transferred blame and emissary victimisation (see Appendix, p. 129). A plethora of Jewish culture theorists, religious and secular, are already explaining and developing Girard's thought, without feeling threatened by his Christian reference (sometimes they agree with it; sometimes they manage to forget it; sometimes there are overt or subterranean tussles, mostly contained by the shared awareness of mimetic rivalry itself). The common anthropological starting point and approach, the manifest usefulness of his conceptual toolset, the dynamic of common inspiration and discovery, stretch a very long way, at all events, in creating a tolerance of ultimate difference.

A further criterion of serviceability is this: when Christian faith listens to the anthropologist who loves it, it acquires just the right combination of humility and the intellectual rigour needed for interfaith dialogue. It has a holy simplicity, which is the most radical – but paradoxically, also, the most generally acceptable – face of human difference. It is acting in the style defined by Jesus himself, when confronted by the dismissive cynicism of Pilate's 'What is truth?' (John 18:38). Truth cannot be adequately spoken or proven by argument and it can never be possessed – only enacted, shown forth. One cannot wish overwhelmingly, at one and the same time, to be right and to be in, of and from the Love divine. Has the religion of the ultimate self-revelation of God, constitutionally and often, forgotten that paradoxical tension, that law of its own incarnation? If so, its faithful disciple, the mere anthropologist, can put it back in touch with its own right mind and its better self.

This is indeed, an open theory: both in terms of non-possessive humility and of hospitable inclusivity, which makes it a natural interlocutor-in-dialogue for many other thinkers in many disciplines. It is also open, finally, in the sense that it has only just begun to develop the horizons of its potential for elucidation, problematisation and understanding in many fields of application.

Leading French philosopher Michel Serres, speaking at the reception of René Girard into the Académie Française, spoke of him soberly as 'the Darwin of the human sciences'. He was hinting that Girard's theory may one day come to be seen as the framing theory capable of coordinating and making sense together of all the human sciences, rather as Darwin's theory of evolution, suitably developed and confirmed, today already coordinates and makes sense of all the life sciences. Girard himself often shied away in discomfort from such pointers to his mega-eminence; which does not necessarily mean that such pointers are misconceived or wrong.

* * *

Perhaps most fundamentally, for Christians (and many others) Girard's platform for intelligent thinking, delivers a more accurate and realistic understanding of their faith, purged of some abidingly pervasive – and divisive – archaic-sacral thinking. Is the same not also true, we may enquire gently, of Coventry's own ministry of reconciliation?

One modest pointer to this possibility: the Coventry motto, as we have noted, edits the text of Luke's gospel. This editing is defensible in Girardian terms, as we have indicated. Nonetheless, the editing leaves those terms and their right reasons unstated, implicit and largely ungrasped (at least in the presentation of its public face and branding). Whereas a clear recognition of that logic is in fact a crucial condition of reconciliatory realism and operational efficacy.

We remember here the telling words of Jesus, which, in the Coventry formula, are, in some sense, edited out, starting with the explanatory and motivating subordinate clause 'for they do not know what they are doing' (Luke 23:34). If human unknowing is a mitigating factor in the eyes of the divine Mercy, then it is also true that the clear-sightedness we come to share with Jesus, and to share more fully, thanks to Girardian theory, will be among the greatest gifts possible and desirable for those who practice reconciliation. Will it not be the case that the more fully we come to a clear-sighted vision of our own human unknowing, the more we will be drawn to and ready for the mission of reconciliation? In learning to read the shadows, we enhance our chances of emerging into the light.

This point can also be expressed with greater urgency: until and unless we see ourselves to be part of the problem – not only, in some general (undefined) sense, but with insight focussed and mobilised by a sharp and pertinent idea of how that is so – we can hardly begin to become genuinely part of the answer. The game called reconciliation is not on until we ourselves speak from something like an identification with the position of the demystifying-forgiving victim.

We dare not fail to notice in the Gospel the immediate and very concrete context of archaic-sacral violence which made it all happen: the Roman crucifixion squad, the lynching crowd, the cruel spectator sport that brought out the vengeful scoffers, the power politics, the complicit or blind misrecognition declared by persons, parties and systems. If we rub out that context, does not something important disappear from view? Do we not lose sight of the hyper-pertinent antecedence of sacred or sacral violence? Do we not fail to discern and to read the logic of founding murder?

On the one hand, the very ancient pattern of human behaviour remains unstated; its universal anthropological resonance undeciphered and unseen. On the other, we lose the singularity of this victim, who is so uniquely in the image and likeness of God that he can change the universal pattern of human behaviour. Here we encounter once more the vertical axis of the Cross, the crucial key, complementary to anthropological understanding, in opening up human attitudes and behaviours.

Only humans willing to recognise their own first nature in the act of archaic-sacral violence can follow that passage, interiorise that metamorphosis; only humans willing to look up vertically to the Cross of Christ are open to receiving fully that likeness which transforms and dynamises the journey of reconciliation.

If this double requirement is elided, the basis of reconciliation is, or risks quickly becoming, an ethical ideal of good intent which we strive to accomplish, while hoping under our breath that the gods, if such there be, will favour our efforts. Worse, if the forgiving Father is then isolated as the only factor in the equation of human response, the petition 'Father, forgive' may even come to take on a persuasion of fatalistic passivity.

The game of reconciliation, in its Christian fullness, we have said, is not 'on' until its participants themselves speak with some degree of dawning identification with, and something approaching a real kinship with, the position of the demystified and forgiving victim. It is not over until positive mimesis replaces all mimetic negativity (true: that point may well be 'Kingdom come'!). In the meantime, reconcilers must speak with a modicum of articulate conceptual understanding of the fractures and black holes to be mended if their message is to carry more weight, and a greater force of contemporary mobilisation, than does the nearly 80-year-old symbol: the blitzed and blackened ruin that will rise from its own ashes.

These are structural requirements. They can, of course, be met existentially wherever reconcilers go to work with a self-positioning forged by suffering and fellow victimhood. This is very much the case of Coventry, whose personnel have the theological acumen and the accumulated experience to flesh out and complete their own founding formulary and to do so in a dozen very effective ways which I have personally seen, heard and admired.

My purpose in referencing (after many others) the iconic founding formula and its silences is solely to highlight the basic enabling conditions of reconciliation. I hope to suggest, most of all, that Girardian theory may be a formidable resource for ensuring that those conditions are met in the fullest sense, and that they will enable a less patchy and empirical – a more strategic and consistent – praxis of reconciliation.

Taking thought with Girard can help us to recognise, refocus and re-energise the potential of the Christian ministry of reconciliation.

6
Taking Thought for Reconciliation

Violence and the sacred is everybody's problem. It is larger and older than we had suspected for, ironically, it is also the problem of everybody. Known or – more commonly, unbeknown – to ourselves, the problem is with us because it is in us; to that extent, we are all 'problematic'.

René Girard, fundamental anthropologist and culture theorist, lays bare the origins and genesis of that problem in terms that make recognisable sense within a post-Darwinian mindscape; yet his diagnosis also retraces, in large measure, the shape of a Christian theology of revelation and new creation. We can say that he validates that shape anthropologically since he confirms from below (using criteria of novelty, symmetry, pertinence and pattern-forming consistency with data) the tenor and possibility of such a theology.

More surely still, Girard sees Christianity as having transformed our culture: 'I propose today that if we are capable of breaking down and analysing cultural mechanisms, it is because of the indirect and unperceived but formidably constraining influence of the Judaeo-Christian scriptures' (*TH* 1987: 138).[1]

---

1. See also *BE* 2010 xiii-iv: 'By accepting crucifixion, Christ brought to light what had been 'hidden since the foundation of the world', in other words, the foundation itself, the unanimous murder that appeared in broad daylight for the first time with the Cross . . . By revealing the founding murder, Christianity destroyed the ignorance and superstition that are indispensible to such religions. It thus made possible an advance in knowledge that was until them unimaginable.' This statement of the world-changing 'singularity' of Christianity has considerable co-resonance with another powerfully counter-cultural statement, albeit now an agnostic one, of the same thesis by historian Tom Holland. See *Dominion: The Making of the Western Mind* (London: Little, Brown, 2019).

In the lesser known wing of his *œuvre*, Biblical texts, anthropologically read, are seen to adumbrate a God who Himself assumes the human problem, in his progressive self-communication to mankind. This self-communication is seen to be liberating and healing: the gifting of a self-knowledge led by love and most fully declared, most transformingly enacted and made available, in the Passion and Resurrection of the Christ. Yet, the Light come into this world in some sense deepens a mirroring shadow . . .

In a Girardian perspective, we now stand in the time of interim-until-completion, in an unfolding present, left open to the play of history and the Spirit-led progression of the Kingdom-that-comes 'on earth as it is in Heaven'. To the eye of the fundamental anthropologist, this interim is made fraught by the fact that the Gospel revelation and its repercussions in history have set running two momentous metamorphoses in human cultural emergence. First, they have liberated the potential of the human creature and his morally ambiguous Promethean energies, so that cultural development has followed a spectacularly accelerating upward curve. Second, by undercutting archaic religion and its sacrificial system, they have increasingly deprived *homo religiosus* (as he strangely remains, even in his desacralised and determinedly rationalistic, self-secularising culture) of his aboriginal failsafe mechanism against catastrophe.

We no longer believe – even though we still practise it a very great deal, in semi-covert guises – that the immolation of emissary victims will influence the powers that make our fate or will restore the human community to life and peace. We are disabused of all transactions of propitiation and/or expiation enacted in the imaginary and symbolic orders. Meanwhile, however, any general conversion of the heart to true light and grace from above seems, empirically speaking, here below, an infinitely difficult and halting progress.

As Prometheans unloosed, we fear for our survival; but, as a species still in the making, we as yet have scant notion of, or care for – let alone trust in and commitment to – the salvation prepared by our Heavenly Father.

The result of this double metamorphosis is that apocalypse – in its archaic definition, beloved of tabloid newspapers, of terminal catastrophe – looms in many self-generated, all-too-human, end-of-the-world scenarios: nuclear war; ecological implosion; the clash of civilisations; wars of the haves and have-nots; the rivalries of regional superpowers or superpower blocks vying for the shrinking resources of a globalised world etc. In Girard's view: 'Our impression of moving into a trap we have set for ourselves will become more acute. The whole of humanity is already confronted with an ineluctable dilemma: human beings must become reconciled without the aid of [archaic] sacrificial intermediaries or resign themselves to the imminent extinction of humanity' (*TH* 1987: 136).

The curious tensions and perils of our own time, together with the travail of the fundamental anthropologist in confronting them, are examined and assessed in the recently published collection of Girardian essays, *Can We Survive Our Origins?*[2] For our present purposes, what we retain from this overview is the context of urgency in which a fundamental alternative, first promulgated in the Gospels, comes to the fore: apocalypse or reconciliation?

Can we, in this extremity, capitalise on the platform of intelligent thinking which the mimetic theory provides? Is it possible to discern how it might be applied, at Coventry and in other like centres and ventures, to bringing back into amity, or at least to detoxifying down to viable levels, the negative mimetic relations which that body of theory offers so fruitfully to diagnose and to alleviate, perhaps ultimately to heal?

* * *

At the most immediate level, that of practical peace-making and peace-building, Girard's understanding of violence and the sacred can offer a model for analysing specific human situations so as to identify and transform their dynamic of malignancy. That case is very ably made in the collection of Girardian essays referenced above, in the section entitled: 'Violent Reciprocities and Peace-building in the Modern World'.

It may not be known widely that the principal input of theory, and a substantial inspiration to creativity in the Northern Ireland peace process, is acknowledged, by leading actors at the Corrymeela Centre for Reconciliation and at Northern Ireland's Council for Community Relations, to have been Girardian. Hence the presence of John,

---

2. See Cited Texts and Further Reading, p. 139. Girard's own diagnosis of the modern condition is perhaps open to criticism in one respect. He advances no theory of mediations, i.e. no concrete vision of the institutional, corporate and other means by which the Gospel message is transmitted to secular culture at large; no definite conception of how the Kingdom yeast rises and works over historical time in the human dough. This deficit contributes to the sometimes abrupt apocalypticism of his later work. It is perhaps the main limitation placed on his reconciliatory usefulness (though he himself would have spoken here of the cobbler sticking to his last).

Lord Alderdice, leading architect and negotiator of the Good Friday Agreement, at the launch of *Can We Survive Our Origins?*, at the Cambridge Festival of Ideas of October 2015, together with Dr Rowan Williams who wrote the Preface.

The best procedure here will be to offer some basic pointers to the practical usefulness of Girardian theory as applied in Northern Ireland and then to leave others to see how far that diagnostic model can be modified and adapted to other situations also evoked in that volume: particularly, South Africa and the Middle East; and the significantly alerting case from which we began the present reflections – the sacred violence of Islamist terrorism. Can we discern something of the shape and potential of mimetic theory which might be applied to these situations and, perhaps, others?

* * *

Mimetic theory helps us, first, to scan the dynamics of conflict and violence in context and to see the nerve-points to be addressed. In the making of the Northern Ireland problem, a number of violently creative forces making the modern world in the sixteenth and seventeenth centuries were concentrated into a postage stamp of disputed territory. The forces in play were: civil war arising from religious and political conflict; the power struggle with Continental Europe, played out within the British Isles; the rise of nationalisms and nation-states. The eighteenth and nineteenth centuries added to these forces the effects of the movement for social revolution.

Two rival communities, each shaped by these forces, and defined overwhelmingly by their mutual antagonism, were condemned by the 'plantation' of Ulster to live cheek-by-jowl, in a relationship of fearful dominance and resentful subjugation; each experiencing its own situation as that of a minority threatened by a larger surrounding Other-majority. Each was deprived of the support of a shared framework of belonging of the type usually provided by nation, state or religion; and each was subject to the same deformed quasi-transcendence – the 'metaphysical' urge to imprint or re-imprint its own identity-image on their uncomfortably shared territorial space.

This potent brew of contextual/situational determinants produced a perfect storm of mimetic rivalry. The two communities were locked into competition at all times and for everything, not excluding control of the territory itself (later, of the quasi-state, or province).

Just as mimetic theory predicts, symbolic and ritual assertions of identity went into overdrive, so as to shore up the permanently insecure identity bond of each part of the conflicted community. Walls sprouted murals of victory and rebellion; pavement kerbstones were painted with identity-marking national colours; parades, with period costumes, pipes and drums, kept the memory of historic rivalry young and its inheritors militantly bonded. Churches (with their sacred places, their theological and liturgical patterns, their authority and their mystique) were recruited, and, in part, subverted, so as to serve each sacred cause; precisely because religion, from the earliest times, has always been most basic form of collective identity-bonding, the most direct expression and the most potent guarantor of its sacred character. Girard's theory teaches us to expect this regression to human origins; and, likewise, to anticipate a concomitant sacralisation of violence and counter-violence.

Nor can it be any surprise that the compensatory turbo of ritual and symbolic identity reinforcement regularly broke down, delivering recurrent mimetic crises of inter-community strife, each with its dynamic of crescendo towards paroxysm; together forming cycles of 'troubles' in which 'rebel' or 'terrorist' violence triggered retaliatory counter-violence and/or state repression.

Meanwhile, the external state sponsors of each of Northern Ireland's conflicted ethnic/religious/national identities held their trustees at arm's length. London was happy enough to bundle up the civil unrest and violence within its jurisdiction into just the one extruded scapegoat community, held largely out of sight, under delegated political control, across the Irish sea; while in Dublin the hyper-identification of the independent state with the Republican mystique of 1916, together with its own pursuit of Irish separateness, produced an inverse, but curiously similar, mirror-image: the same self-protective 'absence', the same Self-ignorance, the same Other-blindness, the same progressive 'undifferentiation' of the rivals (in short, Girardian 'misrecognition' in all its forms).

It was, all-in-all, a well-crafted prison of negative mimesis, further reinforced by long political indifference and economic neglect by the controlling state power at Westminster, and by partisan interventions from the two sponsor governments. This whole devil's brew of trapped and warring identities was further veiled from sight by vague self-justifying myths: English ones about gratuitously warlike tribal Irishmen and the incomprehensible misdeeds of religion; Irish ones about perennial persecution by the larger neighbour and the sacralisation of identitarian exceptionalism, struggle and martyrdom.

What changed in the 1980s and 1990s? In the first place, the geo-political context and the strategic stakes. Britain no longer had an imperial backdoor to guard so jealously; both the British government and the Irish RepublicanArmy (IRA) saw that neither could prevail by force of arms. The Republic of Ireland discovered prosperity thanks to the European Economic Community (then European Community) and stood down from its crusade of nationalist unification. The creation of a new overarching identity framework in the European Union transformed the problem of self-sacralising, Other-demonising local identity politics; and it opened up the prospect of an alternative, more de-stressed and more integrated, future. Mimetic theory, at that point, helped to decipher the patterns of history-in-the-making, thereby discerning the coming time of opportunity.

Above all, it indicated that the key question of the future status (i.e. the state-belonging) of Northern Ireland should – if it could not be taken altogether out of the equation – at least be displaced to the margins and put on hold, while other deficits – of political equality, of social justice, of economic development – were addressed. The European Union provided that overarching holding space of common belonging; it allowed and encouraged economic and commercial cooperation between the rivals and their sponsors. What changed – and mimetic theory helped discern this change, and to engineer the political process of transition adjusting to it – was the framing context.

Thirdly, mimetic theory helped to model the reversal of negative to positive mimesis, from suspicion to acceptance, from rivalry to cooperation, from warring division to peaceful community. Those are the hard yards made at Corrymeela, and at scattered elsewheres, working with individuals from both communities, who told their stories, ducked under the adversarial myths and Other-demonising, sacred memories on either side, and so learned to see their neighbours as avatars of themselves. Reconfiguring attitudes and relationships within small groups, they were modelling the new social and political structures of tomorrow.

Then came the time of opportunity-consolidation, carrying forward the momentum generated by the encounter of a 'carrying' context and the hard-won effort of 'conversion'. This phase was memorably promoted by external honest brokers (the Clinton White House and its peerless chief negotiator George Mitchell) without which (and whom), there could have been no breakthrough agreement and no endorsement of it by all interested parties.

Even then, the marvel of the Belfast Agreement of 1998 was necessary. Its marvel lay in its judiciously contrived balance; its recognition of diverse dimensions; its creation of appropriate processes, facilitating institutions, guarantors; its even-handed generosity in offering something for everybody and hope all round. It was also a marvel of judiciously sequenced progression, bringing into being over time a difficult process of mutual trust, thus providing for the democratic resolution, in realistic sequence, and in due course, of the intractable underlying structural problems.[3]

The former director of Northern Ireland's Council for Community Relations, Duncan Morrow, concludes: 'A good part of the way has been illuminated by René Girard. At the heart of the mimetic hypothesis is the rediscovery of relatedness as the core of human existence. Not only does everything and everyone exist in relationships, but relationships are foundational to being, rather than the other way around. Freedom from mimetic desire, new and positive mimesis is something that breaks in, and, like its opposite, spreads contagiously. . . . The potential consequences of a world mediated by a relationship to the victim are literally revolutionary . . . ' (Antonello and Gifford 2015a: 186).

It will be sufficiently apparent from this recapitulative description of the reconciliatory process why the Belfast Agreement, signed on 10 April 1998, Good Friday, has ever since been known as the Good Friday Agreement. By free consent, it turned around a cruelly snarled and ancient dynamic of bad mimesis and sacred cause. It broke the archaic fatality of eternal recurrence, opening all protagonists up to the truth and the hope fundamental to both sets of warring Christians.

* * *

For my own part, I would wish to endorse Girard's legacy in very much the same terms as Duncan Morrow and this understanding suggests to me that workshop-type peace-building needs to be well-prepared, by small groups modelling larger reconciliations. It strikes me, that this implies a prior, proactive, experimental-theoretical thinktank function: i.e. an activity that is not event-driven, nor even

---

3. It is this delicately engineered architecture and this historic new hope, so hard-won and so fragile, that the time of Brexit threatens to throw into reverse gear. It will be apparent in the coming five years whether a return to the troubles can be avoided, and, in the next fifty, whether the logic of violence or that of co-operation will shape the next phase of Irish history.

narrowly situation-driven and, especially, not driven by institutional self-promotion (which can all too easily take over the best intentions) but is, instead, disinterested, forward-looking and strategic.

We need to take thought for reconciliation at the level of exploratory Other-dialogues, identifying the stress points that the present age of human cultural development generates, modelling problems and responses, gathering-in, with like-minded Others, diagnostic insights and therapies, procedures, tactics and strategies.

This agenda, I shall be told (and am prepared to believe), exists fragmentarily in many forms and places. True enough, but with a far lesser presence and action than the many thinktanks of sectional political and/or ideological affiliation. My proposal here – which is more akin to a strategic approach, than to a project or programme – is that it is called to engage us increasingly, and in an increasingly methodic way, at Coventry, for example, to be pursued in conversation and in concert with other bodies, within and outside the Cathedral and diocese.

Within: because the imperative of 'loving the Lord your God ... with all your ... mind' is, perhaps, the least understood and limply followed dimension of the 'great commandment' and constitutes, as such, a real challenge to the most ordinary Christian practice. Outside: because the dimension of shared understanding is the one we most vitally need to generate, with like-minded Others, in this time of secularisation and of interfaith. In the light of Girardian theory, which is the most inclusive of lights, this seems possible in ways not previously available.

The symbolic value of the renaissance of the blitzed cathedral, and of the petitionary prayer, 'Father, forgive', might find here a more fully incarnate response. Girard's voice, giving value to other voices and establishing a general framework of anthropological understanding, would powerfully aid the unfolding of the Christian meaning of reconciliation; helping to model it as precisely as may be, as widely as may be and in its fullest embodiment.

Let me conclude, then, by sketching out what I think René Girard can contribute to two fundamental dialogues which, so it seems to me, are called for in respect of our problem of 'violence and the sacred'; dialogues that we could and should participate in and should help to promote, if we are to model relationalities and structures, policies and politics, practices and attitudes; dialogues that will help carry us through the fast-globalising and multiply perilous world of tomorrow.

* * *

The first challenge of reconciliation – the first task of ours, if we will have it so – is to engage in an interfaith dialogue on the relations between violence and the sacred. What we're looking for is a comparative and agreed psycho-social poetics of natural human sacralities and of their age-old association with violence. We need to examine together and understand together where violence comes from (how it arises in the collective mind, under which political and social conditions) and what relation sacral violence sustains with religion, as we have previously come to understand it, within our respective faith traditions. The same agenda would then enquire what resources those same traditions can call on to undo what Girard opens up, for the first time, to clear sight, namely, the foundational complicity of violence and the sacred.

In *Not in God's Name* (2015) Jonathan Sacks has already given a lead in this direction, saying that such concertation is quite indispensable to the battle of ideas, of hearts and minds, which must be engaged and won against politicised religious extremism – the greatest peril, he thinks, of the twenty-first century. True enough; though our remit, I would wish to suggest, should extend beyond the battle for hearts and minds to include the reconciliation of hearts and minds within the larger, non-violent and mainstream, faith traditions. Moreover, with the same remit, it should be extended rapidly, to the other Abrahamic faith, which is quite central in the perspective indicated, that of Islam. Then also, surely, to all-comers in the world's major faith traditions. (We would start that second-phase series, would we not, from a viewing together of the film *The Life of Pi*?)

I have indicated how I think Girard's work can take us to the very heart of wounded/wounding difference between the two traditions of Judaism and Christianity, of the two central paradigms of reference currently explored by each – the Shoah for Jews (our contentiously named 'Holocaust'),[4] the Cross for Christians – become no longer stumbling blocks opposable, by each party to the other, in distress, fearful fascination and vengeful irritation, but, instead, a combined resource of clear common thinking and mutually encouraging goodwill: we can, if we are brave enough and faithful enough, seek in common a conversion from bad to good mimesis.

---

4. The reference to a sacrificial burnt offering carries with it (for Jews) the same mystified and perverse archaic-sacral associations as does (for Christians) the clamour of the Passover crowds baying for the blood of Jesus.

We have Northern Ireland and Israel to compare and contrast. In *Can We Survive Our Origins?*, Scott Atran, who is of Jewish descent, recalls Isaac Deutscher's celebrated parable of the founding of Israel in 1948. A man whose house is on fire, jumps out of a window and lands on a local passer-by, grievously smashing all his bones. 'Why did you do that to me?' screams the victim. 'I had to', screams back the victim. In that double victimhood (for fire, read persecution, emissary victimisation) lies the peculiar complexity of this oldest and most central of conflicts. Hence, the redoubled mimetic fascination, the crescendo of symbolico-ritual and actual stone-throwing, rising periodically, cyclically, towards, paroxysm. Maximal readiness to sacrifice the Other generates in turn those advanced forms of negative mimesis we call religious fundamentalism, political radicalisation, extremist violence and so on, cyclically. That's before we begin to factor in the role of conflicted sacralities and the deeply unfavourable evolution of the geo-political context of the Middle East, also describable in terms of negative mimesis.

The real culprit in the Sacks scorebook is the binary moralism of identity politics, an outlook that sacralises a hyper-purified version of Ownself and demonises a blackened Enemy-Other, inducing regressive behaviour and leading to some of the worst crimes in history: pogroms, witch-hunts, mass murders (in Cambodia, in Bosnia, in Rwanda, in the Stalinist Soviet Union, in Maoist China). Pathological moral dualism makes us (i) de-humanise and demonise enemies and (ii) claim victim status for ourselves to justify our Other-victimisations. When dehumanisation and demonisation are combined with a paranoid or perverted sense of Ownself victimhood, stage three becomes possible: the commission of what Sacks calls altruistic evil. Even the extermination of the Enemy Other is then presented in morally and aesthetically ennobling terms – as sacred duty, conferring a light of glory. 'I am doing the Lord's work' (as Cromwell said in Ireland).

All this is amicably close to Girard, at least in terms of group dynamics; though, we notice, without the notion of evolutionary inheritance of an 'archaic sacred' towards which we all are capable of 'regressing'. Sacks' scientific references are to psychology (Freud and Klein) – he speaks in terms of 'sibling rivalry', 'splitting' etc. – rather than by invoking fundamental anthropology and the actual genesis or coming-to-be in history of *homo sapiens*. He agrees with Girard that our ideas of the natural are influenced by our notions of the supernatural but he does not proceed down that open road; nor does he see how it might be a two-way street and a reciprocal movement.

He admits to a specialised, and perhaps restrictive, focus on the fearsome problem of political radicalisation, setting aside any more general commitment to elucidating the problematic relations between violence and the sacred as such. Interestingly, Jonathan Sacks rarely uses the category of 'the sacred' at all and, when he does so, there is little to distinguish it from 'the holy'. Does Sacks, perhaps, in the process, also tend to equate religion with the Abrahamic monotheisms? (His Cromwell example fits perfectly well into a Girardian mapping of the problem; but how, I wonder, would my Irish Druids from Croghan fit into Lord Sacks' picture?)

Girard, it seems to me, casts the net more widely and delves deeper. Thanks to his pioneering work, still little known and poorly understood in this country, we can come to understand a great deal more than we did, about 'violence and the sacred'. If we understand that the internet multiplies electronically the innately viral contagion of human desire itself, we understand at once the role of internet communication in enhancing the sense of a closed and immediate fraternity of sacred cause that has demonstrated its power to draw together in Syria and elsewhere *jihadis* from far-flung Muslim lands. That factor, together with the sense of historic depression affecting Islam, and the sudden salvational deliverance seeming to appear with the Caliphate, explain sufficiently its dramatic recruitment potential, unseen since the International Brigades headed off to fight in Spain in the 1930s.

We know so much more now than we did about the psycho-social dynamics of human rivalry, conflict and violence. A Girardian lens will make us see patterns of reciprocity, where we previously thought of violence in unilateral terms: for instance, the reciprocity between laser-guided smart weapons, launched from 37,000 feet in a campaign of 'shock and awe' and the poor man's riposte in that self-same genre – namely, the suicide bomber; or the mirror-image of sacred violence following the original Muslim conquest of the Middle East and North Africa, encroaching into Europe, and the riposte of Christendom in the holy war of the crusades. This latter – post-millennial – encounter with Islam was the event that most pushed Christendom away from its non-violent roots in the Gospels; and something not dissimilar seems to have happened internally, as Christendom (i.e. the theocratic socio-political entity of that name, sometimes carelessly confused with the 'Kingdom of God') broke up in the sixteenth and seventeenth centuries.

Understanding such things, we are capable of better understanding also the reversibility of the dynamic of crescendo towards paroxysm. Literally, the infernal dynamics of enmity, estrangement and Other-victimisation are the obverse of a heavenly dynamics of other-hospitality, inclusion and acceptance. In one way or another, we have to learn to cast our Kingdom net on that other side of the human boat.

At which point of understanding, it becomes clear that this Jewish-Christian dialogue cannot manage without its Muslim interlocutor. It will be a more difficult interfaith dialogue for including him (for the moment, probably 'him' – but this too is shifting!). A Jewish-Christian understanding-in-principle is not difficult to imagine: if scapegoating and sacrifice are the heart of the matter. If we can together read the books of Genesis, Leviticus and Job (on the afflicted just man, pursued by his accusers in the name of a monstrous divine double drawn from their own substance) and Isaiah (the so-called 'fifth Gospel') on the tender love of God for his people and his project of Messianic restoration, then we have substantial common ground for exploration.

Such common ground may be more difficult to come by in the case of Islam precisely because the scapegoat reflex operates there, more influentially and with a lesser degree of recognition than is the case in Judaism. It operates actively, when the devil is stoned at Mecca, and negatively when the prophet Jesus is held to have been switched for a scapegoat double as the victim of human crucifixion.

As Robert Caspar points out, Islam pursues a different objective of redemption: that of instituting on earth a God-ruled human polity of the type that Christendom once supposed itself to embody (Caspar, 1980: 62). Given Islam's strictly-minded (rigorist) approach to questions of authority and truth in religion, the entire problem of violence and the sacred is still looking for its truly self-critical moment and its adequate formulation. Even so, the dialogue of Michael Kirwan and Ahmed Achtar shows how the most apparently divisive themes can provide the best common ground and the most valuable new light (See Kirwan and Achtar, 2019).

Can we speak together of a God who is not, overwhelmingly, Almighty? Of a reconciliation operating beyond the point of revolt or non-submission (we think of Job); or developing from the brokenness of the Cross? It may be possible if we remember the enlightened practices of cultural toleration have often prevailed *de facto* under Islamic rule. For instance: in mediaeval Islamic-ruled Spain and in many provinces of the Ottoman empire the 'millet' system of community representation allowed minority faith communities to practise their religion without interference, and avoided the large-scale pogroms and persecutions of mediaeval Christendom.

It is also true that the manifest evil of Daesh/IS is challenging Islam on precisely these most delicate points. For its sacred cause, and its own good name, Islam wants and needs to accede to an adequate formulation of the link between violence and the sacred. Only so can it challenge genuinely and strategically the gross confusion, as Muslims often see it, made by Westerners between the mediaeval throwback-fundamentalists of that self-styled organisation and today's mainstream Muslim believers. Only so can it achieve justice for its people, seen by Muslims as victimised historically by the imposition of systems, models and norms associated with Western power. It is not, clearly, that other powers, more recently, have abstained from fishing in the same troubled waters. The reconciliatory point, however, is the importance of being willing to discover the shadow cast by one's own actions – of correcting Girardian 'misrecognition' – and renouncing the sacred causes of yesterday.

The common ground Islam can find with its siblings of the other Abrahamic faiths is the notion of Allah the All-Merciful. The most strategic terrain of theological discussion might be how that Mercy is enacted and how it effects transformation in the socio-cultural order (but also, then, in world process and history). The most promising opening towards bi-lateral understanding might perhaps, in Girardian terms, be the common recognition that we are all engaged in blame transfer, that nobody has a monopoly of emissary victimisation, and that the sacred and the holy are to be distinguished. That will be a longer discussion, almost certainly, perhaps without foreseeable term. However, can we suppose that beginning it is any less important than is the other (Jewish-Christian) dialogue; can we think that it is less required or less potentially worthwhile?

Something else Girard contributes distinctively to both faith dialogues: our scientific, post-Darwinian secular mindset is constantly reminding itself of the continuity of man with other animals; whereas human violence is, in fact, different. Humans take offence and seek revenge. They fight against disproportionate odds. Defeated, they come back for more. Uniquely in the animal world, they care about affront or injustice suffered as much as, sometimes more than, any physical damage sustained. Their animosities, their resentments, the intensity and resilience of their rage are those of Other-interested animals, intimate with Others, engaged with Others.

All this because of the mimetic faculty itself which also allows us to cooperate so supremely well. Girardian mimetic theory explains brilliantly why sacred violence must be considered – not as the opposite of our altruism and cooperation (as cognitivist socio-biologists so frequently take it to be) – but as the concomitant face of our very capacity for altruism and for intimate other-relatedness, its shadow side.

Once we see the deep-seated connection of opposites, we can envisage a sun-blessed reversal or turn-around. Every party to the interfaith dialogue can envisage it, moreover, since it will apply (albeit differentially) in each religion (and none). Not only so, but believers and unbelievers alike can participate in and contribute to this enterprise, providing only that all are able and willing to enter into the same self-examination in a spirit of reciprocity.

From the beginning, Girard insists also that the ultimate form of rivalry in humans – of conflict and violence too, therefore – is metaphysical: we compete, not for any limited good or goods, but, ultimately, for ground-zero ascendency in the matter of identity. From Girard, we know that what turbo-charges specifically human violence is that self-generated sacrality which mysteriously goes with the sense of collective identity; a sacrality that is both Other-demonising and Self-divinising; thus, making it so much more devastating, irreparable and apocalyptic than is animal violence. Monotheists should not miss that hint, any more than should Eastern theosophists. The tiger is in us, for sure, but the question must then always be: to whom does the Tiger belong and in which places and cultural contexts does he live?

The obvious point at which to begin these very crucial interfaith deliberations on violence and the sacred might be the case of the Holy City of Jerusalem, brilliantly evoked by historian Simon Sebag Montefiore. 'Jerusalem is the universal city, the capital of two peoples, the shrine of three faiths; it is the site of Judgment Day and the battlefield of today's clash of civilisations. How did this small remote town become the Holy City, the 'centre of the world' and now the key to peace in the Middle East? . . . The only city that exists twice – in heaven and on earth' (Montefiore 2011).

This coveted, prized and disputed Holy City, where the three Abrahamic faiths all pray, and which is foundational for each, has been multiply conquered and occupied, destroyed and rebuilt throughout its history. It has been more fought over than any other city; yet each faith, when it held ascendancy here, has 'borrowed from the sanctity of those Others who came before'; 'the more destroyed, the more revered' (Montefiore 2012).

Is this the most complex and delicately critical, therefore, of all cases of violence and the sacred? A sort of recapitulative case, an epitome of Girard's foundational complicity in action? Having read Girard, we are full of questions about this case which is still awaiting appropriate framing and adequate conceptual formulation, questions best addressed, at all events, in common, by all the concerned parties.

Does 'sanctity', in Montefiore's presentation, mean 'sacrality' or 'piety', i.e. the sacred common practice of a tradition and culture of religious faith? Or does it mean 'holiness', i.e. actual, recognisable Godlikeness? If the latter hypothesis is taken to be an accurate statement of the case, why, then, is the history of the Holy City such an unholy history? That question, if not evaded or short-circuited – as it usually is, most frequently by blame transfer – must be something of a game-changer.

Why did this Holy City become the object of such violent rivalry, vividly documented by Montefiore, over the entire period of Jerusalem's history? How, too, in the modern period, did it become infected by such apocalyptic religious fervour (was that element, perhaps, always latent from the beginning?).

What do we think of Montefiore's final formulation of the 'problem' of Jerusalem, its 'paradox' as stated above? Does it summarise well what he himself has shown previously? What ambiguities of the word religion are involved? To what extent can we agree that the borrowing of elements of religious tradition and practice from a religious Other a sign of hope?

Jerusalem seems to be an enlarging, heightened, even apocalyptic, mirror to interfaith relations, as a whole, and to the role in human affairs of religion, as such. If so, is that because it illustrates so well, and illuminates so profoundly, the foundational complicity of violence and the sacred, and does so without obvious recourse to the sacrificial non-solution of eliminating the category itself of religious truth?

I do not anticipate that such questions will rapidly bring agreement! Swift common understanding is hardly to be expected, if we are indeed looking at: (i) the *locus classicus* of the three religions of divine self-revelation; and (ii) at the most central knot formed of the most ancient and entangled roots linking human violence and the sacred. If we wished to construct a concrete model of two or more hands – not always the same hands – reaching out for the same object (that object being the greatest possible Object of human desire), it would be difficult to invent a more instructive case-history. Nevertheless, 'after Girard', mutual understanding, mind gearing with mind and, perhaps eventually, heart meeting and matching heart does seem to be in principle possible.

We may be sure of one thing: when once the faithful of all three religions concerned simply begin to address – seriously, advisedly and together, invoking both anthropology and theology – these very questions, there will be a dawning hope of reconciliation, locally, in the Middle East, and for humanity at large. Perhaps, then, Armageddon, and all 'final battles', foreseen as being enacted for Jerusalem, on the nearby coastal plain of Megiddo, may modulate into relationships of a more liveable, peaceful and creative difference. We shall at least have learned than it is not 'difference' that separates us, but the mimetic rivalry we have in common . . .

* * *

If we allow our thinking to be directed by such measures of pertinence and significance as those just outlined, then it follows also that our dialogues of reconciliation may, should and must engage, on the other hand, with the secular mind – with agnosticism and even with atheistic humanism.

The liberal-democratic West, as it pursues its path of secularisation, continues to lose contact with its religious roots. How then will it still manage to discern the evolutionary logic of the sacred within itself; and distinguish this from a logic that is truly holy? How will it not remain prisoner of its 'rational actor' models of conflict and peace-making, lifted straight from the boardroom and the industrial disputes tribunal? How will it manage to surmount its own uprooted shock-horror at the brutalities of fundamentalist extremism; and how will it come then to avoid the 'shock-and-awe' riposte, from 37,000 feet, mimetically answering the fundamentalist crusade of the suicide bomber? How shall we not become, in the very moment of asserting most strenuously our difference, monstrous doubles of those whom we condemn and combat?

Girard helps us enter into this secularist dialogue. He envisages and integrates, in a way Darwin never did or could, science and religion. How many other first-rate minds have grasped the nettle of spelling out the complementarity Girard sees between evolution and Judaeo-Christian revelation? How many secularists – and how many scientifically-minded theologians – have, since Darwin, understood that interface; or even attempted to renegotiate it seriously? What would happen tomorrow if people of faith and people without it were to come together in the understanding of that interface?

If, everywhere, today, we run into the same Girardian problematics of mystified and self-sacralising human violence, with its actually or potentially apocalyptic horizons, that is because sacred violence is enfolded deep within our social psyche, in our institutions, our myth-making and our practices of intra- and inter-group relations; so that those realities of origin haunt us still. We are inhabited and shaped continually by them.

What we may reasonably hope for, however, is that, by scanning modern cultures with a Girardian lens, we shall get very much better at discerning the residual shadow of inherited archaic-sacrificial thinking, sensibility and practice within our own modern societies. Believers and non-believers can join forces in that task.

There is a striking example of this in the collection of Girardian essays *Can We Survive Our Origins?* The supposedly Christian United States is there considered as an 'Empire of Sacrifice'. The title of that study invokes – provocatively – a book on the Aztecs (Carrasco's *City of Sacrifice* 1999). Everyone knows about human blood-sacrifice as practised in pre-Columbian Mexico and we are all are happy enough to recognise that phenomenon, as long as it remains safely confined somewhere else. Alas, archaeologists increasingly know that it was not and that it cannot be so confined. Too many avatars of Croghan Man have been discovered, in most human cultures, just about everywhere around the globe.

More challenging still, however, to our own culturally reinforced persuasions of innocence is the story of how, just next door, in 'good old US of A', a certain strand of Reformation theology, has been made to justify a culture of 'innocent domination' and even 'innocent violence': from the Puritan wars against the Native Americans, through the epics of internal and, then, external US expansion, up to George Bush's War on Terror and the killing of Bin Laden, passing via Bible-belt 'creationism', megachurches, the gun cult and the righteous filmic violence of the classic Western.

Did we ever wonder why violence is 'as American as apple pie'? Or whence came the TV reality thriller *Homeland*; or Dylan's protest song 'With God on our side'? What we are seeing, in situations of displacement, of stress and hyper-mobilisation, is an ever-possible resurgence of the archaic foundations. In modern minds, in modern cultures – alive and well – there is a black economy of *archaic* sacrifice.

* * *

In short: the same logic of archaic-sacral sacrifice that helps us understand fundamentalism and political radicalisation within an Islamic culture-sphere, also deciphers a vast swathe of dark matter within our own culture-sphere, within historic Christendom and within the secular atheism of today's progressive liberal democracies.

So that for consequent readers of René Girard, there isn't really anywhere blame-free for anyone to take refuge. We have, henceforth, no real alibi. We just have to help each other tactfully with the negotiation of that human impasse. Tactfully, and, if we are Christians, penitentially, since turning again is the beginning of the path that leads individuals, personally, and then communities of persons, towards reconciliation.

Yet, with penitence comes a very great hope. The ultimate thing we learn from Girard's understanding of violence and the sacred, is that reconciliation is God's own work; the most strategic business running through the whole process of creation and redemptive new creation.

When Satan 'falls like lightening', it is so that man in the image of God may arise, reborn; and the greatest peril then indicates to us – as in the Gospels it does to the Son of Man[5] – the greatest and most momentous of possibilities.

Bon courage, therefore, from René Girard. It's up to us now. Let's take it, thoughtfully, from here . . .

---

5. In Hebrew or Aramaic, this simply means 'mortal' or 'human being'; in later Judaism, 'I' or 'someone like me'. The NT phrase is closely linked to Daniel 7.13, where 'one like a son of man' is brought on the clouds of Heaven to 'the Ancient of Days', being vindicated after suffering and given kingly power. Jesus was able to use the phrase as a cryptic self-designation, hinting at his coming suffering, his vindication and his God-given authority (Tom Wright, Glossary, *Luke for Everyone* [London: SPCK, 2014]).

Appendix
'From Animal to Human', 'On Religion'

Conversations with René Girard,
conducted at Stanford University, Palo Alto, CA in April 2009
by Pierpaolo Antonello and Paul Gifford

Editor's note: some minor editorial interventions [in square brackets] have been inserted to clarify René Girard's thought or make explicit its logic and continuity.

R.G. René Girard / P.A. Pierpaolo Antonello / P.G. Paul Gifford

'From Animal to Human'

R.G.: Lucien Scubla[1] has his own definition of me: I'm the positive conclusion of a project now abandoned by most people, because they thought it impossible to accomplish, i.e. the anthropological programme of the late-nineteenth/early-twentieth centuries, aiming to arrive at a unified science of man, which would explain the transformation involved in hominisation, i.e. the passage from the monkey to organised, specifically human, societies. This is what mimetic theory essentially is.

The last representative of that abandoned programme was Freud. I'm some sort of anti-Freud; and yet close to Freud as well in the type of answer I give. Freud, too, starts off from a collective murder . . . that's the beginning of society as a whole.

But I'm an amateur; I'm not a professional field-anthropologist. That's enough to turn off a lot of anthropologists . . .

Girard and Darwin

P.G.: Do you remember your impressions on reading Darwin's *On the Origin of Species* [1849]?

---

1. French-Jewish sociologist, author of works on Lévi-Strauss and partner in a longstanding dialogue with Girard.

R.G.: I was full of admiration. This was the sort of book I would like to have written. It had a formidable unity. I was aware that mimetic desire could become for collective psychology, for human relations generally, the simple unifying factor, capable of being developed in many directions – perhaps appearing contradictory, but reconcilable at depth – and which would have the same kind of unifying virtue, linking up biology and culture.

I show the scapegoat as the resolution of the crisis involved in this transformation, the crucial and explanatory missing link. But to suggest I grasped fully the deeper compatibility of the two theories would be excessive.

P.G.: The difference between evolutionary theory and mimetic theory is that your theory is re-centred on the notion of the human animal as essentially *homo religiosus* . . .

R.G.: Yes. Something has changed, I think, in the reception of Darwin. Darwin doesn't really get into human culture, or religion, except in a very schematic way. . . . He didn't dare to. He was so convinced, so early, that his theory had atheistic consequences. . . . He glimpsed from afar what he feared would be the devastating effect on his wife's quite basic religious convictions and drew back. He didn't discuss these implications even privately. He was convinced that his theory was going to destroy his wife's naive belief; there's one letter where he says he is so sorry for her! . . . He doesn't see that, as soon as you have man, religion is *the* essential fact in evolution. These days, I'm far from being the only one to see that (I perhaps have better means for dealing with that fact). But there is an evolution of culture which is an is essential part of evolutionary emergence of man and needs to be integrated [into a single theory of hominisation, bridging the gap between animal and human, nature and culture].

R.G.: I see [at work in this process of theorising evolutionary emergence] a sort of modern puritanism, which consists of refusing human superiority. I accept very fully that human being comes out of the animal, yes, but he/she is different. And that difference is far from being insignificant . . .

P.G.: Yes. That's an important part of the notion itself of evolution. As subject and actor of history, man acquires an ever more predominant role in the coming-to-be of things [cf. 'Genesis']. Yet the modern reception of Darwin's theory has tended to be levelling: we tend to assume that the fact of being part of Darwin's single 'tree of life' must make man merely an animal? One animal among others . . .

R.G.: Yes, and that's not true! Though Darwin himself [as opposed to many Darwinists] is, if you look closely, more complex, the superiority of man is constantly present to him; he grasps the many-sidedness of his theory [e.g. he expresses awe, in the last pages of *Origin*, in contemplating the beauty and stunning diversity of life forms].

P.G.: And then, Darwin's big idea, unsurprisingly, also escapes Darwin . . . He didn't quite see the reach and implications of his own theory. What does the word 'evolution' mean to you, René? I'm not at all sure the word is used in the same way in English and in French. In English we usually speak, not of cultural evolution, but of cultural development [which tends to make it separate from 'biological evolution']. And yet what is suggested by the bringing together of your theory and Darwin's is that evolutionary emergence operates at both biological and cultural-ritual levels.

R.G.: Yes. Sacrifice evolves/develops in such a way as to provide a protection from violence. That's the paradox of sacrifice. A [therapeutic or pharmacological] dose of violence protects us from violence. The paradox of violent blood sacrifice is that it means less violence, not more [it reduces the potential for generalised and incremental violence in human communities]. . . . People who declare themselves hostile to my theory generally see it as making man more violent than he really is . . .

P.G.: Especially if they view sacrifice through the prism of a modern ideology descended from Rousseau. Man is naturally innocent and harmonious, until society comes along and corrupts him?

R.G.: Yes, Rousseau never says a word about sacrifice! He never really accounts for it as a mechanism inbuilt into humanity regardless of religion, requiring to be understood if we are to understand the humanity of man. That would be anti-Rousseau [against the grain of his thinking]. He's full of worthwhile insights elsewhere. You could write a thesis on what he considers the positive part and role of culture, the part independent of religion. That anti-religious reference is not visible on the surface but it's quite powerful in him. He would certainly judge me too favourable to religion!

P.G.: Would he ever have imagined the flexibility of your theory? The way it accounts for the conversion of the destructive power of human mimetic desire and rivalry into a force of invention, stabilising the social community, and enabling super-violent humanity to live together, despite being as violent as we are? [See *TH* 1987: 87.]

R.G.: Well, Rousseau is against any tricky mechanisms like that. He wants to explain things simply.[2]

2. This demand for simplicity, when the matter at hand is complicated, is a frequent

P.G.: In one sense, however, your theory is the simpler of the two: you see the power of destruction already present in animal communities, without any moral implications at that point, and then super-volted in human ones [by virtue of our greater capacity for mimesis, which also commands our greater skills and intelligence]. So far, so simple. But then, thanks to sacrifice, that destructive potential is converted into a civilising force; albeit ambiguously so, since our animal antecedents are still programming. We inherit violent predatory instincts; we rise up out of violence, as it were, and stand upon it. It's always already there and we never quite get free from it . . .

R.G.: For the modern age, Rousseau is very important because he thinks religion is a useless complication of something that should come about without it, namely the good and positive aspect of culture.

P.G.: Goodness being natural, whereas we have to explain everything else?

R.G.: Rousseau, you know, is fundamentally speaking against the Christian idea of original sin. This is something so profound in him that he doesn't necessarily know it but, even when he does it unawares, he is, fundamentally, speaking against original sin. And my theory is really the opposite of that. It says there is original sin in culture itself; although culture also shows a defence mechanism against its worst and most destructive effects. Original sin protects you from the worst consequences of original sin . . .

P.G.: Archaic sacrifice as the [fortuitously formed but elective] self-defence mechanism of the sinful creature? . . . And it's clear from your work you think Rousseau has many descendants: not least the ethnologists and anthropologists of the Victorian and early-twentieth-century periods.

R.G.: Our century has been fundamentally acquired [*sic*] to Rousseauistic assumptions.

P.G.: And is Dawkins one of those thinkers?

R.G.: Not, I would say, when he considers the straightforwardly evolutionary aspects of culture; but, when he talks about violence and religion, he certainly is. Most scientists hold a Dawkinsite view; not all, but many. Today most people realise that evolution and creation are not

---

cause of frustration. An interesting example is given in S 1986: 117-21. Girard answers the objection made against his hypothesis on myth: myths, it is said against him, are silent about scapegoats. That's just the point, he argues back: they cannot thematise what is in fact the generating and controlling point of their own structure. . . . That's what makes them *myths*.

simple or simply opposable concepts. They aren't always sufficiently aware of this problem, however, for them to question the supposed anti-religious thrust of Darwin's theory. What's extremely naive in nineteenth-century thinking about and around Darwin is not to realise that religion, from the beginning, has something vital and foundational to do with the origins of man and the organisation of human societies. . . . [These Rousseau-influenced thinkers] didn't want to go down that road. They had a purely philosophical view of religion. You can see this in Auguste Comte.[3] In Comte there are three stages of cultural development: first, the religious (which is purely irrational, magic), then the metaphysical (which is more rational and a bit less stupid), then, finally, comes the advent of nineteenth-century science . . . Most moderns exist mentally within that ideologically determined reading of history.

P.G.: Is that still Dawkins' view?

R.G.: That's still Dawkins' view . . . that's why he's extremely naive.

Homo Imitativus

R.G.: Whenever philosophers and scientists have taken an interest in imitation, it is usually from a negative viewpoint: it's something imitative, therefore not original – something banal and commonplace. Hence, its relative unpopularity. Scientists have sometimes been interested but with an overly limited idea of what imitation is. My very simple discovery is that, if we can imitate everything, we also imitate the desire of the Other. Our greatest imitations are inspired by those we most esteem and admire. But to desire the same thing introduces pretty quickly a principle of rivalry, which is the great enigma of imitation. Aristotle never saw this; he never took it into account. Intellectuals don't like to talk about it, despite or because of the fact that their research activity makes them, professionally, specialists-in-competition! The more you grasp the mimetic principle, the better able you are to develop a critique of our psychology, of our sociology . . .

P.G.: It's when you apply mimetic theory to deciphering the underlying logic of genesis [the generative logic] that links nature to culture and which drives hominisation that you enter a truly Darwinian stream of thought? Basically, you're interested in animal antecedents; you look back in evolutionary time across the gap between animal and human, trying to see what sort of process produces the passage from animal to human, from nature to culture.

---

3. Auguste Comte (1798-1857), French founder of sociology and of philosophical Positivism, author of the 'three ages of man' theory.

R.G.: Yes. People say monkeys imitate. But it's not true. They don't imitate that much. The most important thing is that animal rivalries are out in the open; they almost never produce mortal combat [between animals of the same species]. One surrenders and the other ceases to be interested in fighting. Wolves lie down and offer their throats, which their rivals refrain from biting. With men, there are no natural limits to mimetic rivalry and violence [the hard-wired instinctual mechanisms of inhibition operating in animals are swamped and overridden]. The limits have to be programmed into them in the form of rules, which are culturally derived and transmitted; and their rivalry is not out in the open.

P.G.: So there are two singularities in your mimetic theory. One is the foregrounding of the problem of violence [which peaks, at the apex of hominisation, in a whole series of mimetic crises]; the other is that you take seriously the role of religion, in its most primitive forms, as a cultural fact.

R.G.: As a cultural fact, yes. Primitive religion is largely composed of two things: prohibitions which are self-explanatory [they are 'don't go there' signals placed on the most likely objects of mimetic rivalry]; and sacrifice, which is what you must have when prohibitions fail [and rivalry produces internal conflict and eventually crisis, and finally the threat of community implosion]. Prohibitions, sacrifice: they are the first human institutions [along with myth, which is the founding identity story of the group or tribe]. Sacrifice is the first and founding human institution, in the sense that killing a member of the community is the failsafe mechanism you must have if and when prohibitions fail. Sacrifice isn't commonsense at all. The sacrificial killing of a scapegoat victim or a surrogate of that first victim – it can be an animal, but fundamentally, at the beginning – it's a human being . . .

P.G.: There's another singularity in your theory: the centrality of sacrifice, which in a sense explains the emergence of all other aspects of culture. Can we get behind these first institutions to what drives them?

R.G.: Perhaps vengeance, which is not an institution, but the cause of institutions. Vengeance doesn't exist in animals. They don't remember; when they stop fighting, they lose interest and forget all about it. Yes, sacrifice is central; not least because it explains the emergence of symbolicity and language, hence the mental capacity for collaborative social organisation. The emissary victim, already involves a complex mental operation. The sacrificial victim stands for, and stands in for, the community as a whole. He's chosen as victim by [delegation and] replacement. The Nua people of the upper Nile today have a kinship system for cows, which reduplicates [sic] the kinship system of the tribe. Every member has a cow named to represent him or her. They kill a selected cow; thereby illustrating the logic of 'emissary' victimisation. We could study the language they use and might gain clues as to the development of human language. [R.G. elsewhere explains the development of sacred cows in India as the forgotten product of a half-completed sacrificial ritual.]

In the act of sacrifice, we have a first statement of the notions of similarity, difference and identity. The victim must be like the person you really want to kill but not the same; he needs to be not your brother but a lookalike. So, a fruitful intellectual operation is involved. You can imagine that several steps are involved in the development of the ritual and in the process of victim selection.

P.G.: So sacrifice is a sort of safety valve or lightning conductor. It is invented to cope with the upsurge in destructive power of human rivalries and conflicts, once hominid animals acquire greater brainpower, better weapons, become hunters and seek revenge. You need a lightning conductor and a safety valve to avoid implosion – to actually survive. The founding murder, particularly the invention of its repetition in ritual sacrifice, is what ensures human survival at the threshold of hominisation and enables the elementary components of culture to be invented and put in place.

R.G.: Yes. And there's something else – from a little later on. Something I haven't yet discussed in print. It's this business of the exchange of gifts [a well-known theme discussed by Mauss, Lévi-Strauss et al.]. In my view this is pure nonsense. It's the modern idea that we are all men of goodwill; so we all want to exchange gifts, don't we? No! This the anthropology of avoidance. You set certain objects and operations apart because your tendency is to fight over them! You fight over your sisters, when it comes to bride exchange. So, you go far away [to seek, e.g. brides, the form of exchange involved in exogamy] to deal with someone who means nothing to you. And nothing to your brother. Someone who's not connected with previous fighting or anything of the sort. And we should understand that the logic of avoidance commands the entire system of exchange. It makes more sense than a sudden surge of mutual benevolence towards someone unknown . . . [See *TH* 1987: 73-79.]

P.G.: So you think ideological prevention, not to say prejudice, has played a considerable and occulting role in the decipherment of human origins?

R.G.: Sure. Why does man go far away to satisfy needs he could more easily satisfy immediately, within the tribe and close to home? Why go remotely to someone unknown? He makes arrangements with the remote guys because they have needs symmetrical to his but not conflicting. It's the people close to us we fight with.
P.G.: Does this apply also and even to the burial of corpses? [See *TH* 1987: 80-83.]
R.G.: Yes. I saw that the language of exchange applies even to corpses. Corpses? Why would you want the other fellow's corpse from the tribe next door? Well, but if you do bury his corpse, you are like a professional undertaker, proceeding without emotion – avoiding the risk of renewed conflict at and around funerals. Archaic tribes knew how to manage that... [R.G.'s point is that archaic societies do not have a 'naturalistic' - modern, prosaic - view of death. Death is sacred and electrifying. As physical decay, it involves the danger of the contamination or contagion of evil (hence prohibitions surrounding corpses). That's one form of sacrality. The other is that the corpse reminds you of the ritual victim of archaic sacrifice. 'The reconciliatory powers of the surrogate victim are responsible for the human discovery that joins, over one cadaver, all that can be called death and all that can be called life' (*TH* 81). Some tribes thought no-one died without becoming a god. It is entirely thinkable that certain corpses could be disputed and fought over for this reason. Particulary if this motive were mingled with vengeful thoughts about who caused the death. Offloading the corpse was sparing oneself the fearsome 'undertaking' of dealing with death *as a sacral reality*.]
P.G.: This goes back at least to the Neanderthals who were the first to bury corpses, I think? It may go back earlier still.
R.G.: Yes, but these datings are all subject to revision.
P.G.: One of the most interesting things. Your theory, in *Things Hidden*, posits that sacrifice is the 'centre of signification' – it conduces to the development of symbolicity and language; it teaches humans to manipulate the world in re-combinable signs and make associations through symbols. Meaning, and the power of making meanings and transmitting them irradiates from this organising centre.
R.G.: Yes. The sacrificial victim becomes a centre of preoccupation and thought, a challenge and a developmental agent of thinking and speech...
P.G.: Have you read any other account of hominisation that strikes you as coping as – or more – successfully with the complications, paradoxes and challenges of hominisation?
R.G.: If I had I would have adopted it!

'On Religion'

P.G.: How far does your theory provide what might be called a 'poetics of religious variety', an account of how religious differences came about, what types there are and how they relate to each other? Do you think it helps the student of comparative religion in any way?

R.G.: Yes, it's a view of comparative religion. Because the religions, although very different in the stories they tell – in the type of evil committed by the god or the good done etc. – they are [at] one in their misunderstood scapegoat structure. Religious diversity has been the major argument against religious truth in the West. When you become aware of the panorama of religions worldwide, you can't believe any one of them – they are all alike. Yes, but then some interpret themselves and some do not. . . . In Vedic thought you have many intuitions that are the same as the Christian ones. You don't have Christ, of course, which does set Christianity apart. But many of the things that are in the Gospels can be reached by other means.

From Mythology to Christianity

R.G.: The mimetic theory acknowledges the fundamental similarity between mythologies from all over the world and the Gospel. Many myths – it would be wrong to say all, since our definition of myth is so vague anyway – begin from a collective murder and present an interpretation of collective murder. The Gospels also fit that definition, and this becomes the basis for the assimilation of the one to the other. It goes back to Celsus [second century CE]. He was the first to detect a similar underlying structure: 'These foolish Christians, they don't realise it's all fundamentally the same thing. The Gospels are obviously mythical.' Yes, there's a similar structure. But, no, it's not the same thing! From this reply comes my definition of myth which is: a myth is a misunderstood scapegoat phenomenon. It describes a real social phenomenon mythically; it's part of the phenomenon of scapegoating, you see, that it is misunderstood by the people who carry it out and who regard the mystified version of it which they themselves generate as true. Whereas the Gospels give us a correctly understood scapegoat phenomenon; a reading which turns against the scapegoaters and proclaims the innocence of the victim. Modern [anthropological] science should have become more aware than it is of this crucial difference. They should at least have read the Gospels and realised that Jesus is regarded as innocent by the disciples, if not by the crowd. . . . In both cases you have a central murder by the collective. Both illustrate the scapegoating mechanism built into human society. . . . But only in Christianity is the victim fully justified. A myth is a scapegoat mechanism, that works [sacralises its own act, thus mystifying the scapegoaters, along with those who read their accounts].

Christianity is a scapegoat mechanism that does not work, in that sense. And, in that sense, it goes against the grain of humanity. . . . But it is consistent with the development of the theme of the sacred and its scapegoating violence as it develops throughout the Bible. Joseph in the OT is scapegoated by his twelve brothers (twelve – that's already a crowd!). Yet he is seen as innocent in the story. Not only does he forgive his brothers, but he forgives his brothers when one of them refuses to enter into the scapegoat trick [of deflected and relocated blame]. Remember, Joseph says, bring Benjamin if you want to receive grain from me. He gives them the grain but then tells them, 'You can go except for Benjamin. He stays here with me.' Joseph doesn't intend to harm the boy but he's testing his brothers [by engineering a scenario of scapegoating analogous to the original one whereby Joseph himself was sold off into Egypt]. Only one, Judah, comes back and says, take me instead [thus acknowledging his own guilt]. Judaeo-Christian texts get to things anthropological that myths will never uncover or show you . . .

You can see the relationship between the Joseph text and the text of the suffering servant. The lynching by the crowd of the suffering servant is acknowledged as prophetic of the Passion; but you can find in the OT a dozen or so more texts standing in this precursor line. People should have worried a bit more about the sheer number of collective murders in mythologies.

Why should we differentiate mythologies from the Gospels? Well, because one interprets honestly and correctly what is happening, and the other doesn't . . .

P.A.: How do you interpret or use the word 'prophetic'?

R.G.: Anthropologically. As the gradual understanding and articulation of the way human societies are set up and perpetuated. In order not to see this, you only have to take the sacralised oracle as some sort of incomprehensible gift from the god, as a saving precept which you repeat blindly without understanding it. [i.e. You are protected – from knowledge as well as from harm; but this non-recognition does at least protect you from greater, more generalised violence.] Archaic religion is also, in one sense true, therefore. Of course, in a sense very much more limited than is the case in Christianity.

P.A.: How important is the historicity of the Gospels?
R.G.: It's crucial. [My whole method is a deconstruction of mystified or mythic elements in worldwide scenarios of origin. In the Gospel, we substantially touch history.] It's an incarnation of the truth. To teach people the truth. To be a disciple of Christ is to understand that the victimary syndrome has been correctly interpreted. . . . But, of course, anti-Christians would not recognise that we are dealing with the [age-old common reference situation], this time correctly interpreted. [The whole of our scientificity, and all our science, however, is liberated, set free, by this insight into founding realities of human common life.] If we understand scientifically, it's thanks to the Gospel. Historicity is enormously important.
P.G.: And the role in all of this of Victorian anthropologist Sir James Frazer [author of *The Golden Bough*]?
R.G.: Frazer is very powerful in the sense that he's the first to use the word scapegoat in a modern sense. Everyone these days talks about scapegoats but few realise that, in the famous first text of Leviticus 16, the modern sense is not there – the victim accused falsely by an entire community. When does it first appear? If you take the *Littré* [the famous French dictionary], it's first used like this by the French historian Saint-Simon, who, writing in the 1820s, writes: 'Mme X is the scapegoat ['*bouc émissaire*'] of her salon.' Meaning: she's being scapegoated by them, but she doesn't know it and they don't know it. In English a similar sense develops at about the same time. But this is a purely Western [post-Christian] phenomenon, as is pointed out by the Japanese scholar Masao Yamaguchi [*TH* 131]. You can't say 'scapegoat' in Japanese; you have to use the English word and gloss it. It's not that no one in Japan had the slightest inkling of anything of the sort [it's just that the scattered and imprecise intuitions never came to a moment of public crystallisation]. So, Frazer is the first to concentrate attention publicly on the modern sense: an act of general and arbitrary victimisation, off-loading blame and punishment. That's pretty late, end of the nineteenth century.[4]
P.A.: How do you interpret that? Why so late?
R.G.: There are forms of understanding that are unconscious, or pre-conscious, but which take a long time to come to the surface and form a consensus of clear usage. [And remember, we have been talking about

---

4. But, see also *S* 1986: 120-21, where R.G. criticises Frazer for limiting the development of understanding by failing to distinguish the rite as such from its victimary mechanism and structure, 'like the whole of the science of his time'.

a self-mystifying, self-protective sacralisation developing around the very deep and sensitive site of our common collective beginnings.] . . . Frazer is the first to understand primitive culture has scapegoats in the modern sense. But he doesn't apply the notion to himself; and he's absolutely sure it's purely and simply an archaic phenomenon! In other words, there are no scapegoats in England in the nineteenth century!
P.A.: There was the – very famous – Dreyfus Affair in France . . .
R.G.: Yes, and that's why I say this case was so important. Important: that a whole country would come to be seen as wrong in its scapegoating; also that the victim would be Jewish, picked out by Christians . . .
P.G.: It was a paradigmatic psycho-drama of the whole nation becoming aware of this archaic phenomenon in the modern world.
R.G.: I would like to write something on this subject. The Dreyfus case is a spectacular one. The whole authority of the state is thrown behind this act of scapegoating, and a whole bunch of people resist, keep fighting for the innocent victim. . . . They didn't [much] use the expression '*bouc émissaire*' but they were very conscious that Dreyfus [was being arbitrarily selected to shoulder the blame and take the hit].
P.G.: Some people, even today, are likely to say this is a purely archaic phenomenon. But then what about the gravest event of the twentieth century, the Holocaust of European Jews? What was this but the scapegoating of an entire people? And which people? With which background, recapitulatively, as victims. . . . The assertion that we are all way beyond this would seem to be subject to extreme caution!
R.G.: Yes, in the sense that most people are certainly not beyond it. But the knowledge of how the mechanism functions and why is today broadly available. That's new. Frazer himself was rejected in his own time. There was something a bit odd about that. People sense that here was something a bit dangerous in his work, a principle dangerous to nineteenth century nationalism and its civic establishment. People said about him that he was a good anthropologist but that 'all this business of scapegoating, such nonsense! – to be expelled from anthropology immediately'. I think that what actually happened in anthropology was in fact the opposite of that . . .
P.G.: Your theory is also a theory of human moral obliquity, isn't it? We're never fully lucid about ourselves morally speaking; we have sideways glimpses which are fleeting. We never view ourselves full-face, full on.
R.G.: If we discover something dangerous, we turn away, offload it. Frazer has become, in fact, the archetype of the self-satisfied anthropologist who looks down on 'primitives'. At the same time, look

at how he began to uncover the scapegoating phenomenon; and, in a way, this was related to that. In getting rid of Frazer, anthropology was dismissing the best with the worst.

What Christ is aware of is that the scapegoat phenomenon couldn't remain the basis of society. Once understood, it became unavailable. In other words, you cannot found the social order on gods sacralised and mobilised by sacrifice. You have to do away with these things. Therefore, one of the most ancient defences of society against generalised violence is gone. Modern intellectuals reading the apocalyptic passages in the Gospels don't remember this and don't like those texts. They seem scary, unfit for modern consumption. They're happy there are no directly apocalyptic texts in John; and they prefer John, as against the Synoptic Gospels, where they are present.

Christianity and Apocalypse

P.G.: What, in apocalyptic writings, is actually revealed or disclosed or unveiled? The hidden foundations of culture; the mystifying delusion of archaic sacrifice?

R.G.: Yes, the scapegoat phenomenon that has dominated mankind, ensuring social peace despite human violence, and this is no longer available as a defence. Most moderns don't understand this; and they don't know much about the New Testament. They think there's only one such text in the NT – in the last book, which has this word in its title. In reality the Gospels reveal the impossibility, henceforth, of the old archaic-sacral foundations of human community; these need replacing. The scapegoat mechanism is unavailable as a foundation; the Temple and animal sacrifice both need replacing.

P.G.: Your understanding of this concept is intriguing. You seem to be taking away from modern religious sceptics and from fundamentalists alike the sense they both really understand, and are fondest of, i.e. the millenarian sense of an end-of-the-world catastrophe, which is the fruit of the wrathful intervention of God, winding up everything.

R.G.: Yes, the End envisaged is here of purely human agency. Not due to the intervention of God. Quite the reverse: 'If the time [of the apocalypse, connoting upheaval, catastrophe and unbearable suffering] had not been abridged [i.e. by God] no one would have been saved' [Matthew 24:22]. Because, no Christians, and nothing of Christianity, would have been left. This doesn't mean abridged by a few days. We're talking about an era of history [which] I identify now as the modern [i.e. post-archaic] era. The end will come sooner than it would have done naturally for that reason. You can consider that the abridgment, in any case, is reckoned by Jesus to be the work of his heavenly Father.

The revelation is of the scapegoat mechanism and of the abyss it opens up. Once understood, it becomes unavailable to us – we are deprived of its protection. Man is stripped of the defensive tool that has always allowed him to protect himself from generalised and paroxysmal violence.

One of the reasons these texts have not been taken seriously, have been seen as 'way-out' and foolish, is that culture and nature are mingled together in the violence. In our world the goal of science is to separate out entirely the violence of nature from its counterpart of human violence. And in the 'little apocalypses' of the gospels, you have the mixture again. But in the modern world, say, the cyclone in New Orleans, it has become impossible to distinguish what nature contributes and what is the role of man. Even scientists say they don't know which is which – which is surprising because modern science prides itself on just that distinction.

Evolution and Revelation

P.G.: I don't know whether you saw the recent BBC programme for the bicentenary of Darwin's birth by Dr Conor Cunningham, a theologian and philosopher from Nottingham University. He quoted from Darwin a sentence to the effect that he [Darwin] saw no ultimate contradiction between a Creator and his theory of evolution.

R.G.: That would have been at the end of his life. He couldn't have said that earlier. That's a possible development a number of people have explored. The Catholic Church originally hesitated. In that position, they typically say: 'We have plenty of time – at least 200 years or so, then let's see.' But the last Pope [Benedict XVI] said that Darwin's theory was 'more than a theory'.

P.G.: Even in an Anglican context – Anglicanism being the official and obvious adversary of Darwin. The Bishop of Oxford expressed the religious objection in the famous debate. Darwin had his sights on the natural theology of William Paley. Darwin's wife was a devout Anglican etc. The debate was really about the worth of the theistic 'proof from design' and the supposed literality of Genesis, i.e. about a form of religion circumscribed in its provenance and, by its acceptance, even at the time. And acceptance changed: Darwin was buried at Westminster Abbey, which would not have been the case had he not won approval from the more philosophically open and religiously confident, such as Charles Kingsley. The real polemic developed in America, where scriptural literalism and fundamentalist theology led to anti-Darwinian 'creationism'.

P.A.: How do you see that debate?

R.G.: I'm not sure I have a general view. Creationism, so-called, never bothered me because there was never any substance in its objection to Darwin. Nothing that could pose a real problem. So, it never really interested me.

P.G.: Isn't that because your theory short-circuited the objection? You never get to the point where any problem arises. You take us round another way. You never look at the order of creation and deduce from it that there is or isn't a transcendent origin and end, a Creator God. No, you say: let's look at anthropology, at man himself, at what religion represents for him and why. Is religion itself evolutionary and evolving? Is it open to transcendent potentials? Is there a point at which these potentials become realised and 'revelatory'? You give us an account of religion which is itself evolutionary; and in which evolution is reconcilable with revelation.

R.G.: What is revealed in my theory is essentially the frailty and falsity of earlier religions.

P.G.: Yes, of the human basis of natural religion. Most people will say: religion is either natural (man-made) or supernatural (God-given). It can't be both! And what your theory does superbly, it seems to me, is to suggest how and why that opposition may in fact be false. Revelation may emerge and be crystallised at certain key junctures of natural, i.e. evolutionary, time.

R.G.: Yes, and that's interesting because at the beginning, when *Things Hidden* was published, I was informed . . . informally . . . that the French [Catholic] bishops were considering meeting with me. Then, the meeting was subsequently cancelled and there were voices going in the opposite direction.

P.G.: You think there was a moment when it was still uncertain whether your theory – let alone Darwin's – were receivable within the Catholic tradition?

R.G.: Yes, sure.

Editor's Note: this is an interesting sidelight on an episode which is described more fully in *Can We Survive Our Origins?* by Michael Kirwan. René Girard's own original definition of sacrifice and sacrificial religion was seen by the French bishops as giving insufficient credit to Christian difference as expressed in Church doctrine. In particular, his critique in *Things Hidden from the Foundation of the World* of the Epistle to the Hebrews was considered over-severe, excessively anti-sacrificial.

This was a two-sided misunderstanding for which Girard has acknowledged some responsibility. He subsequently amended his position, partly under the influence of his correspondent and fellow decipherer of *Violence and the Sacred*, Fr Raimund Schwager of Innsbruck University. The fairest conclusion long-term might be his own remark about the dense and darkly gleaming enigma contained in the keyword at the centre of his work: 'the word sacrifice is used to designate archaic rituals and altruistic self-giving, two diametrically opposed things' (*QCC* 1994). As well as any other, this insight epitomises the seminal breakthrough of understanding in Girard's work.

Cited Texts and Further Reading

Referenced works cited in the text are recognised by indications of author and date. In the case of René Girard, this practice is supplemented by initials indicating the particular editions and translations listed below: *BE – Battling to the End*; *DDN – Deceit, Desire and the Novel*; *EC – Evolution and Conversion*; *J – Job: The Victim of His People*; *QCC – Quand ces choses commenceront*; *S – The Scapegoat*; *SFL – I See Satan Fall like Lightning*; *TH – Things Hidden from the Foundation of the World*; *VR – La voix méconnue du reel*; *VS – Violence and the Sacred*.

Alison, James, *Raising Abel: The Recovery of the Eschatological Imagination* (first published 1996) (London: SPCK, 2010)
———, *The Joy of Being Wrong: Original Sin through Easter Eyes* (New York: Crossroad, 1998)
Antonello, P., and P. Gifford (eds), *Can We Survive Our Origins? Readings in René Girard's Theory of Violence and the Sacred* (East Lansing, MI: Michigan University Press, 2015)
———, *How We Became Human: Mimetic Theory and the Science of Evolutionary Origins* (East Lansing, MI: Michigan State University Press, 2015)
Barberi, M.S. (ed.), *La spirale mimétique* (Paris: Desclée de Brouwer, 2001)
Bataille, Georges, *Erotism: Death and Sensuality* (*L'Erotisme* [Paris: Editions de Minuit, 1957]), trans. Mary Dalwood (San Francisco, CA: City Lights, 2001)
Bergen, Peter, *Holy War, Inc.: Inside the Secret World of Osama Bin Laden* (New York: Free Press, 2001)
Burleigh, Michael, *Sacred Causes: The Clash of Religion and Politics, from the Great War to the War on Terror* (London: Harper, 2005)
———, *Earthly Powers: The Conflict between Religion and Politics from the French Revolution to the Great War* (London: Harper Perennial, 2006)
———, *Sacred Causes: Religion and Politics from the European Dictators to Al Qaeda* (London: Harper Collins, 2007)
———, *Blood and Rage: A Cultural History of Terrorism* (London: Harper, 2008)
Carrasco, David, *City of Sacrifice: The Aztec Empire and the Role of Violence in Civilization* (Boston, MA: Beacon Press, 1999)
Caspar, Robert, *Pour un regard chrétien sur l'islam* (Paris: Editions du Centurion, 1990)

Cyrulnik, Boris (ed.), 'Faut-il imiter pour exister?', *Sciences Psy*, no 14 (Juin 2018)
Darwin, Charles, *On the Origin of the Species* (London : Arcturus Publishing Ltd, 2017)
Esposito, John, *Unholy War: Terror in the Name of Islam* (Oxford: Oxford University Press, 2002)
Frazer, J.G., *The Golden Bough* (London: MacMillan & Co., 1910)
Freud, Sigmund, *Totem and Taboo* (London : Taylor & Francis, 2nd new ed., 2001)
Gifford, Paul et al. (eds), *2000 Years and Beyond: Faith Identity and the 'Common Era'* (London: Routledge, 2003)
Girard, René, *Deceit, Desire and the Novel: Self and Other in Literary Structure* (*Mensonge romantique et vérité romanesque* [Paris : Grasset 1961]), trans. Y. Freccero (Baltimore, MD: Johns Hopkins University Press, 1965)
———, *Violence and the Sacred* (*La violence et le sacré* [Paris: Grasset,1972]), trans. P. Gregory (Baltimore, MD: Johns Hopkins University Press, 1977, 1979)
———, *Things Hidden from the Foundation of the World* (*Des choses cachées depuis la fondation du monde* [Paris: Grasset, 1978]), trans. S. Bann and M. Metteer (Stanford, CA: Stanford University Press, 1987)
———, *The Scapegoat* (*Le bouc émissaire* [Paris: Grasset, 1982]), trans. Y. Freccero (Baltimore, MD: Johns Hopkins University Press, 1986)
———, *Job: The Victim of His People* (*La route antique des hommes pervers* [Paris: Grasset, 1985]), trans. Y. Freccero (Stanford, CA: Stanford University Press, 1987)
———, *Quand ces choses commenceront. Entretiens avec Michel Tréguer* (Paris: Arléa, 1994)
———, *I See Satan Fall Like Lightning* (*Je vois Satan tomber comme l'éclair* [Paris: Grasset, 1999]), trans. J.G. Williams (Maryknoll, NY : Orbis Books, 2001)
———, *La voix méconnue du réel. Une théorie des mythes archaïques et modernes* (Paris : Grasset, 2002)
———, *Battling to the End* (*Achever Clausewitz. Entretiens avec Benoît Chantre de René Girard* [Paris: Carnets Nord, 2007]), trans. Mary Baker (East Lansing, MI: Michigan State University Press, 2010)
———, *Le sacrifice* (Paris : Editions de la bibliothèque nationale de France, 2015)
Girard, René, and Gianni Vattimo, *Christianisme et modernité. Entretiens menés par Pierpaolo Antonello* (*Verità o fede debole* ? [Massa : Pier Vittorio e Associati, Transeuropa, 2006]), French trans. Renaud Temperini (Paris: Flammarion, 2009)
Girard, René, with Pierpaolo Antonello and João Cezar de Castro Rocha, *Evolution and Conversion: Dialogues on the Origins of Culture* (Edinburgh: T & T Clark, 2007)
Girard, René, André Gounelle and Alain Houziaux, *Dieu, une invention?* (Paris: Les Editions de l'Atelier/Editions ouvrières, 2007)
Guillebaud, Jean-Claude, and D. Peccoud, 'René Girard, décrypteur du sacré', *La Croix*, vendredi, 5 novembre 2015, pp. 2-3
Hitchens, Christopher, *God is Not Great: How Religion Poisons Everything* (New York: Twelve, 2007)
Hodder, Ian (ed.) *Violence and the Sacred in the Ancient Near East. Girardian Conversations at Çatalhöyük* (Cambridge: Cambridge University Press, 2019)

Holland, Tom, *Dominion: The Making of the Western Mind* (London: Little, Brown, 2019)
Juergensmeyer, Mark, *Violence and the Sacred in the Modern World* (London: Routledge, 1992)
———, *Terror in the Mind of God. The Global Rise of Religious Terrorism* (London: Routledge, 2003 (2001)
Kaplan, Grant, *René Girard, Unlikely Apologist: Mimetic Theory and Fundamental Theology* (Notre Dame, IN: University of Notre Dame Press: 2016)
Kirwan, Michael, *Girard and Theology* (London and New York: T & T Clark Continuum, 2009)
Kirwan, Michael, and Ahmed Achtar, eds, *Mimetic Theory and Islam. The Wound where the Light enters* (London: Palgrave Macmillan, 2019)
Kristeva, Julia, *Histoires d'amour* (Paris: Denoel, 1983)
Lewis, C.S., *Miracles* (1947) (London: Collins Fount, 1976)
Lorenz, Konrad, *On Aggression*. Translated by Marjorie Kerr Wilson (London: Routledge, 1966 [1963])
Mahoney, Jack, *Christianity in Evolution: An Exploration* (Washington, DC: Georgetown University Press, 2011)
Mann, Charles, 'The Birth of Religion', *National Geographic*, June 2011, pp. 34-59
Martel, Yann, *The Life of Pi* (Toronto: Knopf Canada, 2001) (Film, Dir. Ang Lee, 2012 [DVD 2013])
Montefiore, Simon Sebag, *Jerusalem: The Biography* (London: Weidenfeld and Nicholson, 2011) (Jerusalem: The Making of the Holy City, BBC DVD, 2012)
Orsini, Christine, *René Girard*, Collection *Que Sais-je?* (Paris: Hachette, 2018)
Oughourlian, Jean-Michel, *Genèse du désir* (Paris: Carnets Nord, 2007)
Palaver, Wolfgang, 'Abrahamitische Revolution, politische Gewalt und positive Mimesis', in W. Guggenberger and W. Palaver, *Im Wettstreit um das Gute: Annäherungen an den Islam aus der Sicht der mimetischen Theorie* (Münster: LIT: 2009) pp. 29-65
———, *René Girard's Mimetic Theory* (East Lansing, MI: Michigan State University Press, 2013 (2008)
Pascal, Blaise, *Pensées et Opuscules* ed. Léon Brunschvicg (Paris: Hachette, 1959)
Perret, Bernard, *Penser la foi chrétienne après René Girard* (Paris: Editions Ad Solem: 2018)
Pinker, Steven, *The Better Angels of Our Nature: The Decline of Violence in History and Its Causes* (London: Allen Lane, 2011)
Ricœur, Paul, and André Lecocq, *Penser la Bible* (Paris: Seuil, 1998)
Sacks, Jonathan, *Not in God's Name: Confronting Religious Violence* (London: Shocken, 2015)
Swartley, Willard M., ed, *Violence Renounced. René Girard, Biblical Studies and Peacemaking,* Institute of Mennonite Studies: Studies in Peace and Scripture vol.4, (Pennsylvania: Pandora Press, U.S., 2000)
Williams, J.G., *The Girard Reader* (New York: Crossroad Herder, 1996)
Williams, Rowan 'Girard on Violence and the Sacred' in *Wrestling with Angels: Conversations in Modern Theology* (London: SCM, 2007), chapter 9
Wright, N.T., *Surprised by Hope: Rethinking Heaven, the Resurrection and the Mission of the Church* (London: SPCK, 2007)

Index

Akedah (the 'binding' of Isaac), 3-5, 68fn
Anthropology, xii, xiv, 1,7,18, 28, 38fn, 43, 59, 61, 62, 66, 85, 98, 114, 120, 129, 134, 135, 137
Apocalypse, 10-11, 27-28,74-75, 83, 91, 93, 97, 99, 106-107, 121, 135-36
Archaic-sacral religion, 3, 4, 8-10,18, 32, 36-40, 81-82;
    reworked in O.T., 62-71;
    in N.T., 74-79, 89, 98, 103;
    residually retained by Israel, 70-71, 74-6;
    by Islam, 116-117;
    residual imprint in Christian thought and culture, 103, 106, 120-122, 125-126, 130
Attenborough, Sir David ,12, 63fn,
Atheism, 12-13, 59, 122
Aztecs, 39, 113
Bataille, Georges, 8
Bradley, Rt Rev Ian, 34fn
Bonhoeffer, Dietrich, 2
Burleigh, Michael, 1
Caiaphas (Jewish High Priest), 83-84
Carnival, 40, 54 . 87
Christianity, 14, 21;
    allusions in *Lord of the Flies* 33-34;
    R.G. and Christianity, 58, 62 fn, 63,93;

Judaeo-Christian revelation and the archaic sacred, 58-61, 62-69;
the Old Testament ('that's how the Light gets in'), 65-71;
gospel context of violence, 72-74;
the Beatitudes, 74-75;
R.G.'s anthropological argument, 91;
gospel cases of sacred violence, 75;
controversy with scribes and Pharisees, 76-79;
Passion and Reconciliation, 83-93, 111;
from mythology to Christianity, 131-35 (see also Frazer);
Christianity as religion-and-culture transforming, 98, 103-104, 105-107, 121-122;
and interfaith dialogue, 113-120;
dialogue with secular humanism, 120;
evolution and revelation, 136-138;
and apocalypse, 135-136;
and original sin, 99-100, 126;
and evil, 64-66 (see Satan)
Choudary, Anjem, 5
Comte, Auguste, 127
Coventry Cathedral, ix-x, 94, 95, 102-104, 112 (see Girard, Reconciliation)

Croghan Man (bog-buried sacrificial victim), 81-85, 88, 92, 115, 121
Culture contemporary cultural situation, xiv, 3, 8, 11, 26, 32; genesis and hidden foundations of human culture, xi, 12, 16, 28fn 36-37, 40-47, 50-51, 60, 67-69, 127-128;
culture of reconciliation, 93-95;
mimetic analysis of culture spheres, 67, 77, 99fn 89, 92, 99, 100, 122, 125, 126, 134
Cyrulnik, Boris, 25
Darwinism, Darwin and Girard, xiv, 123-127;
the Darwinian 'crisis', 63, 64 fn, 136-137;
mimetic theory and group intelligence, 24-28, 31-32, 47-48;
bridging the animal-human divide, 43-47;
recognising human specificity, 34, 51-52, 62-65, 43-47;
evolutionary theory and mimetic theory, 120-121;
Girardian perspectives: post-Darwinian mindscape, 35, 105, 117;
survival is not yet salvation, 11-12, 21, 31-32, 64 fn, 64-65;
the new beginning of Genesis, 62-63, 66; evolution and revelation, 136-137
Dawkins, Richard, 13, 59, 126-127
Dennet, Daniel, 13
Durkheim, Émile 52
Esposito, John, 1
'Founding murder' master concept, 17, 22; prefigured in Golding, 28-34; in Freud, 35-37; as foundation of religion and culture in Girard, 37-57;
involving mimetic crisis, 37;
'resolved' by victimage mechanism, 36-38;
generating ritual blood sacrifice, 38-40;
generative principle, 41-43;
bridging nature and culture, 43-45;
as evolutionary legacy structuring human psyche, 50-51;
epistemological status, 47-51;
at Göbekli Tepe, 51-57;
case of Croghan man, 81-83;
resurgent in the modern world, 118-120;
'invisibility' of founding murder, 40-41, 59, 63 (see Misrecognition, Myth);
untombing of things hidden, 67, 79 (O.T.), 72-76 (N.T.),81, 85, 90, 103, 105fn, 129 (Passion);
'founding murder' transparent to Jesus, 76-78;
the Cross as replay of 'founding murder', 83-89;
yet 'abyssally different', 86;
and Reconciliation, 93, 95
Francis (H.H. Pope), 11
Frazer, Sir James, 28, 85, 133-135
Freud, Sigmund, 28, 35, 36, 51, 59, 89, 114, 123
Fundamentalism 'Islamic State', x, 1-2, 5-6, 13, 25-26, fn, 68, 92, 120, 121, 138;
and mimetic theory, 45-46, 68-69;
and archaic-sacral religion ('regression'), 5, 12-14, 31-32, 53-56;
potential declared by the crucifixion in everyone, 84;
including Christians, 98, 99;
and Jews, 114, 120-122;
central to conflict over Jerusalem, 118-119
Göbekli Tepe ('world's oldest temple') subverting anthropological perspectives, 52;
design, 54;
associating violence and the sacred, 53-57;
sacrificial rites, 54-55;
the enigma of perpetual fine-tuning and rebuilding, 55-56;

Index

unlocked by Girard's theory?, 57
Genesis, 3, 9, 17, 18, 21, 22, 50, 51, 61-65, 67,100fn, 116, 124, 136
Girard, René, ix;
and French Theory, xi;
and Girardians, xii-xiii;
critical *mésestime* in Britain, xiii-xiv, 66, 86;
Catholic reception, 16-17, 137-138;
and the theologians, x, 5, 66;
Christian apologist and critic, 58, 98, 99, 136;
anthropological approach to biblical texts, 16, 61-66;
and to doctrine, 87, 99-101;
personal faith, 58fn;
intellectual project, 42-43, 44, 71-72, 76-80, 106-107, 117-118, 121-122, 123 (see also Sacred, Violence deciphered);
contribution to theory and practice of Reconciliation, 101-102;
and to Northern Ireland peace process, 111;
enabler of required fundamental dialogues of reconciliation, 112-122
Harris, Sam, 13
Haykel, Bernard, 6
Hills, Rev Dr Sarah, ix-x,
Hitchens, Christopher, 12-13, 14, 59
Hodder, Ian, 48-50
Islam, Islamic, 1, 2, 6, 13,15, 18, 20, 26, 27, 75, 113, 115, 116, 117, 122
Judaism Hebrew scriptures ('how the Light gets in'), 65-71;
radical honesty in facing sacred violence, 71-80;
residual 'founding murder' in historic Israel, 75-79, 80-84;
operative in both Shoah and Passion, 79;
key to transcending antisemitism and uniting to meet the challenges of violence and the sacred, 113-114;
the case of Jerusalem, 115-118; 122fn (see also J. Sacks)

Kirwan, Michael, xii, 17fn, 137, 138
Kristeva, Julia, 8-9
Lewis, C.S., 87
Lévi-Strauss, Claude, ix, 40, 129
Lord of the Flies, 29-34, 84
Mimetic theory, mimesis and 'imitation', 22-34, 127-130;
mimesis positive, 24-25, 86, 111;
and negative, 32, 109, 114;
the mimetic triangle, 32, 62-65, 65;
mimetic rivalry, 26-27, 32-33, 63-66, 73-74 [cf. *lex talionis*] 100, 101, 108-109, 119;
mimetic 'scandal' (see Satan), 80, 100;
mimetic crisis, 28-31, 36, 40, 54, 67, 84, 86, 109;
grounded in metaphysical identity-assertion, 26, 33, 94-95, 108, 118;
runaway dynamic of crescendo towards paroxysm, 31-32, 54, 73-74, 84, 97, 109, 114-115;
mimetic reversibility, 55, 88, 95-96, 98, 99, 107-122, 113;
turbo-charging group intelligence, 10, 28, 40-41, 60;
creating 'monstrous doubles', 25-26, 31-32, 55, 84, 97, 109, 110;
in evolutionary perspective, 124-125, 127;
theologal mimesis, 63-64, 87-88, 96
Morrow, Duncan, 111
Misrecognition (*méconnaissance*)
uncertainty gap, 5-6;
cognitive and moral blindness, 33, 42, 50, 78-79, 88-89, 100-101, 103, 109, 117;
invisibility of founding murder and myth, 40, 48-49, 56fn;
aversion ('denial'), 43-44;
opening up the tomb of self-misrecognition, 77-78;
'they know not what they do', 86-89;
deconstruction of human self-enfoldment within violence, 90-92;
recognition and reconciliation, 91-92, 97-99, 100-101, 111, 121 (see Original Sin)

Myth (mythologies) as sacred identity narratives, 40, 42, 50, 51, 67-68fn;
  Girardian poetics/hermeneutics of myth, 16, 21-22, 35-36, 40, 42, 61, 121, 126fn;
  myth and religion, 33-34, 42, 60-61, 67-68fn, 70, 131-135 (see Misrecognition)
Passion (of Christ), xiv, 4-5, 13-14, 15-16, 63, 72-73, 74-78;
  replay of 'founding murder', 83-87;
  yet 'abyssally different', 86;
  reversing archaic sacralisation, 86-87;
  dispelling human self-misrecognition, 88-89;
  connecting to 'every ritual on the planet', 85-86;
  redefining sacrifice and 'making the archaic sacred archaic', 88-89;
  enabling Resurrection, showing the divinity of Christ, 88-89;
  and revealing hidden things, 90;
  the 'mousetrap theory' of atonement, 92;
  'I see Satan fall like lightning', 90-93;
  transforming conception and practice of 'salvation', 'conversion', 'apocalypse', 'martyrdom', 92;
  making Reconciliation possible, 93-122
Pinker, Steven, 11-13
Nietzsche, Friedrich, 28, 39, 40, 51, 59
Life of Pi, The, 19, 21, 22, 113
Reconciliation paths towards, i, 2-3, 15, 16-17, 19, 37;
  first-form: around the victim, 47;
  the Light gets in, 61, 66, 67, 71;
  defined in gospels, 93-94;
  assumed the Passion, 92;
  thought out on two axes, 95-96;
  Christian Gospel as inclusive matrix, 96;
  bringing penitence and empowerment, 90-92, 93-95, 122;
  Girard's fruitful platform of intelligent thinking: taking the measure of the problem, 97;
  spotting the operative fulcrum, 98;
  deconstructing fundamentalist culture shells, 98-99;
  enabling the mimetic reversal (negative to positive), 98, 100-102;
  liberating from cultural shadows and mimetic doubles, 95-101;
  setting a truth-and-reconciliation ethos 101-102;
  conferring a 360 degree self-and-other recognition, 97-103;
  useful at Coventry?, 102-104;
  in Northern Ireland peace process, 107-110, 111;
  requiring thinktank function, modelling future dialogues of Reconciliation,112-122
Religion as ambiguous category, x, xi, 1-2, 3-4, 6-7;
  proto-form and residual lining: the sacred, 7, 14-17, 17-18, 19-20, 108-109, 113;
  the 'foundational complicity of violence and the sacred', 118-119;
  Girardian frame of understanding, xi, xiv, 3-5, 58-61 (types), 113-116, 132-133 (man-made *and* God-given);
  'First form religions' (see Archaic sacral religion);
  Abrahamic religions (see Judaism, Christianity, Islam);
  World religions, 19-20;
  Vedanta scriptures, 60 (see also Mythologies);
  Religion as matrix and crucible of human development ('*l'humanité fille du religieux*'), 32-33, 34, 42, 44, 46-47, 50-51, 52-56, 132;
  organised around a more or less violent disavowal of human violence, 40-41, 77, 79 (see Sacred, Violence);
  and Judaeo-Christian revelation, 7, 33-34, 87-88, 98-99

Ramsey, Michael, 87
Resurrection, 17, 34, 72, 76, 82;
   and the sole transcendence of Love, 83;
   anthropological focus and 'bow wave', 85-88;
   and divinity of Christ, 86;
   and reconciliation, 89, 91-92, 95
Ricœur, Paul, 17
Rousseau, Jean-Jacques, 43, 125-127
Satan: deviated transcendence, serpent cunning and Genesis, 63, 63fn, 64;
   maker of mimetic 'scandal', 78;
   subject of the system, 100;
   'I see Satan fall like lightning', 90, 122
Sacks, Jonathan, 15, 17, 113-115
Sacred 'dark matter', protean, 2;
   changing, 3-6 (see *Akedah*);
   a binding-bonding super-us-ness, 7-10 (see 'group intelligence');
   dark and luminous forms, 7-8;
   major player, 8-10;
   sacred violence as proto-form of human spirituality (the 'sacralising animal'), 9;
   the process of sacralisation, 32-34, 37-40;
   foundationally based on violence misrepresented, 38, 49 (see Misrecognition, Myth);
   poetics of false sacralisation ('deviated transcendence'), 37-41, 62-64;
   regression, 5, 14, 84, 109;
   tit-for-tat, 24, 25, 74;
   sacred rage, 75, 90;
   lapidation, xiv, 75;
   lynching, 32-33, 36, 39, 84, 103, 132;
   projections of a 'monstrous double', 32, 33, 65, 70, 71;
   the tangled roots of violence and the sacred, 78, 79-80, 98-99, 109, 115;
   the sacred and the holy, 6, 78, 119, 114-115, 121 (see Archaic-Sacral Religion, Violence)
Sacrifice child sacrifice, 3, 5, 33, 65;
   and eroticism, 8, 33, 65;
   and victimary process, 32, 39-41, 53, 55, 66, 69, 75-76, 83-93, 99, 116-117, 121;
   specified as ritual blood sacrifice, 37-41;
   sacrificial catharsis and Greek tragedy, 38, 40, 54, 71;
   as protection against violence, 39, 55, 121;
   as generating origin of culture, 41-43;
   modulation of sacrifice, 4, 71;
   case of Croghan man, 81-83;
   sacrifice redefined by Passion (see Passion);
   we live in sacrificial societies ('enfolded' logic of blood sacrifice), 85, 90, 98, 121
Scapegoat, scapegoating ('emissary victimisation'), 16, 33, 109;
   expressing the logic of blood sacrifice, 36-41, 49, 44, 55,78, 83, 84-88;
   involving blame transfer, 69, 71, 117, 119;
   and lapidation, xiii, 32, 75, 133-135;
   in Judaeo-Christian scriptures, 62, 69-92, 75;
   theme for Jewish-Christian dialogue, 15, 116;
   scapegoating misunderstood, declared truthfully, by degrees understood, 60, 69, 90, 92, 101, 131-136
Schwager, Raimund, 138
Serres, Michel, 102
Transcendence socially generated, 5, 7, 8;
   perceptible in ritual sacrifice, 18, 21;
   deviated transcendence, 18, 21, 63, 65, 108;
   vertical (divine) transcendence in gospels, 86, 91
Victim of sacrifice, 4-5, 33, 37-8;

sacrificial ritual, 39-41, 49, 54, 56fn;
  involving sacralisation
  (divinisation), 38-39;
  identified as universal signifier,
  founding the symbolic order, 38fn;
  founding first-form reconciliation,
  47;
  victimage mechanism, 36-37, 41-
  42, 49, 51;
  victimary process, 38;
  animal and human victims, 31-33,
  54, 69;
  the victim figure as rebel (Job), 70-71;
  as saviour (Suffering Servant), 71-
  72, 114;
  Christ as emissary but forgiving
  victim, 80, 81-86, 87, 94, 97-101;
  victimisation, the obverse of
  reconciliation, 111, 121
Violence and the sacred, foundational
  complicity, 1, 2, 4-5 (see *Akedah*);
  human violence different, 117-118;
  we are nature's super-Tigers, 11,
  19-20, 21-22, 31, 42, 118;
  contemporary analyses, 11-17
  (see Burleigh, Esposito, Pinker,
  Hitchens, Sacks, Girard);
  self-generated apocalypse, 11, 28,
  68, 99, 106-107, 118, 135-137;
  myths of violent origins (Genesis,
  Life of Pi), 18-20, 21-24, 28-31;
  dynamics of violence in mimetic
  theory, 26-28;
  illustrated in Girardian 'founding
  murder', 35-55;
  edited out in myth (see
  'Misrecognition'), 35fn, 56fn, 44 ;
  'contained', 36, 40-41, 50;
  but permanently interiorised
  and recycled ('embeddedness in
  violence'), 69, 79, 81, 88, 101;
  sacrificial violence ultimately
  impotent, 55-56, 90;
  sacral violence untangled
  progressively in Judaeo-Christian
  scriptures, 67-72;
  endemic in gospel context, 72-73;
  the Beatitudes and sacred rage,
  74;
  gospel instances of sacral violence,
  75-76;
  founding murder transparent to
  Jesus, 76-79;
  Crucifixion as sacral violence, in
  the logic and pattern of founding
  murder, 81-83, 83-86;
  the Cross of Christ as fulcrum,
  converting sacred violence to
  reconciliation, 86-96, 112;
  undoing the foundational
  complicity, 92, 94-96, 103-104,
  110, 119, 121-122;
  refounding archaic sacralities
  in the transcendence of Love,
  89, 92, 107, 103-104, 122 (see
  Reconciliation)
Voltaire, 13
Weil, Simone, 16
Williams, Dr Rowan, xiii, 3, 108
Wright, N.T., 64, 87, 122fn